Real Estate Campgrounds

REAL ESTATE CAMPGROUNDS

How to Invest in Outdoor Hospitality with Campgrounds, RV Parks, and Glamping

Heather Blankenship

BiggerPockets®
PUBLISHING
Denver, Colorado

Real Estate Campgrounds: How to Invest in Outdoor Hospitality with Campgrounds, RV Parks, and Glamping
Heather Blankenship

Published by BiggerPockets Publishing LLC, Denver, CO
Copyright © 2024 by Heather Blankenship
All rights reserved.

Publisher's Cataloging-in-Publication Data
Names: Blankenship, Heather, 1984-, author.
Title: Real estate campgrounds : how to invest in outdoor hospitality with camp-grounds , RV parks , and glamping / Heather Blankenship.
Description: Includes bibliographical references. | Denver, CO: BiggerPockets Publishing, LLC, 2024.
Identifiers: LCCN: 2024933264 | ISBN: 9781960178190 (paperback) | 9781960178206 (ebook)
Subjects: LCSH Real estate investment--United States. | Real estate development. | Camp sites, facilities, etc. | Personal finance. | New business enterprises--United States. | BISAC BUSINESS & ECONOMICS / Real Estate / General | BUSINESS & ECONOMICS / Personal Finance / Investing | BUSINESS & ECONOMICS / Investments & Securities / Real Estate | BUSINESS & ECONOMICS / Real Estate / General
Classification: LCC GV191.72 .B53 2024 | DDC 647.947309--dc23

Printed on recycled paper in Canada
MBP 10 9 8 7 6 5 4 3 2 1

DEDICATION

To my children,
Arabella, Ezra, Ariana,
Leighla, and Lilyana!

TABLE OF CONTENTS

Section I
THE WHY AND HOW OF PURCHASING RV PARKS

Section II
UPGRADES AND ULTIMATE EXPERIENCES

Section III
OPTIMIZING OPERATIONS

INTRODUCTION

L et's go on a journey together. By the end of it, my goal is to leave you energized, educated, and equipped to start on your own path. And if I am able to do that, I'll be fulfilled, and my job as your guide will be complete.

This journey is purchasing and running an RV park—and it changed my life. While the experience has given me many joyous high points, I won't tell you that everything was easy or that I never took a wrong turn. With this book, I intend to tell you about the joys of owning an RV park, as well as the challenges you can expect. By sharing both, hopefully your path will have fewer pitfalls and wrong turns than mine and have more enjoyable moments and opportunities for profit.

Of course, there's nothing wrong with potholes and wrong turns. Some of the most important things I've learned started with a wrong turn. But setbacks can disrupt the journey a bit, and for some, that can be discouraging. I hope to help you avoid those setbacks by being prepared for all that can transpire when purchasing, operating, and maintaining an RV park. Section I will cover the why and how of purchasing an RV park. I'll take you through a brief history of RV park and campground living to give you a baseline for the activity. We'll discuss the varying types of RV parks available and how the type of RV park you choose will attract different kinds of people. All of this is in the spirit of helping you be informed when starting your RV park property search.

Next, I'll shed some light on how to find and fund RV park deals. There are multiple ways to approach an RV park investment, including buying a park as is or building one from scratch. There are certain factors you need to consider, and I'll help set up your search criteria based on those considerations. I'll give you some key things to consider as you approach closing on your RV park.

In Section 2, we'll dive into the potential upgrades and experiences you can offer your RV park guests. We'll expand on the different types of accommodations and activities you can provide, in addition to hosting activities and events (and some legal considerations too). I'll also share some lucrative side hustles you can incorporate into your park to add additional income and heightened customer experiences.

The final section will get into the nitty gritty of operating the RV park. Once the groundwork has been laid regarding why you want to run your park and what you want to offer, we get into the how. We'll cover managing your RV park and running the park itself (including setting up reservation systems, marketing your park to guests, and the day-to-day operations). This section will cover customer service and ways to maximize your RV park. We'll explore some options for outsourcing to professionals in certain special cases.

And last, but not least, we'll focus on your mindset and how to persevere through the many challenges that come with owning and operating an RV park. I believe your mindset is an essential aspect of owning a business, and if you aren't tending to that, your happiness and success will be heavily impacted.

Hi—I'm Heather, and I'll Be Your Guide

I'm a mother of five amazing kids, and I'm blessed to own a business that allows me to spend time watching them grow up. Thankfully, I will not be one of those who declares from their deathbed, "I wish I wouldn't have worked so much," because I get to structure my days as I like, and that means I spend as much time as I want with my children. I wish the same for you, and I believe the blueprint I describe in this book will get you there.

But this isn't about children, per se. Whether you have a significant other or you want to invest in yourself rather than put time in at a nine-to-five job, owning an RV park gives you freedom and flexibility. Those are priceless.

Perhaps just as importantly, this isn't about being lazy and just cashing checks that come in. I think about my investments every day, and I think about how to improve them. I look at new properties, and I work some seriously long hours.

The difference is I decide how many hours I work, and I decide which obligations come first; and those decisions determine how much money I bring home. I absolutely love those three aspects of owning my own business, and I can't imagine working for someone else again.

How did I get to this point? It was somewhat of an accident. Or perhaps it was meant to be. To borrow a phrase from Tony Robbins, it depends on whether you believe things happen *to you* or things happen *for you*. I'm in the latter camp.

A few years back, I took a cross-country RV trip from Florida to California. After staying in several campgrounds and appreciating what each had to offer, I found myself thinking, *This wouldn't be a bad business to own. It's just a bunch of parking spots, right? What could possibly go wrong?*

It turns out plenty can go wrong, but I didn't know that yet. If someone had pointed out only the negatives to me, I might not have taken the plunge. Luckily, that didn't happen, and by the time we arrived in California, I had already looked up campgrounds in my home state of Tennessee and found one that was in bankruptcy.

I was 26 years old at the time and hadn't inherited any family money. But I saw several national headlines about foreclosed properties and people in bankruptcy due to the market collapse we had just gone through. So I thought, *Why not? Let's see what the bank will offer me.*

When I called the bank and they asked me how much money I had as a down payment, I told them the truth: nothing. But those were extraordinary times, and banks had more inventory than they wanted. Plus, banks will readily admit they have no business running an RV park. (What bank executive will answer the call when a sewage line backs up?) With those facts in my favor, I was approved for a $3.2 million loan with no money down.

Spoiler alert: No one will give you that kind of a no-money-down loan these days. You could say I was lucky, or that life happened *for me*. But don't let a lack of resources make you think you can't own an RV park.

My First RV Park

I bought the park sight unseen. In case I haven't stated the obvious yet, I knew nothing about running an RV park—or any business, for that matter. I also happened to get pregnant during the same month I bought the place, and I spent the first two months of RV park ownership sleeping on the office floor and shoveling mulch around the park. (I'm certain I did not make my obstetrician proud.) But I gained one very important thing: I learned how to run a campground the hard way. And sometimes, that's the best way.

I laugh as I think back to how naive I was. I was excited and thought of the RV park as a fun project, but I got a rude awakening when I saw refrigerators strewn throughout the park and mailboxes hung in the craziest of places. The tenants were paying $300 per month, and that covered their site rental, electricity, water, and everything else. No matter how I looked at it, this business had been poorly operated, and there was no way I would make money keeping things as they were.

I had to remind myself: Things happen *for* me.

Instead of becoming overwhelmed, I decided to look at the positives. This park was attached to Dollywood, of Dolly Parton fame. That gave it enormous potential. Plus, the neighboring areas were far more attractive than the one I bought. I essentially purchased the cheapest house on the block, which can absolutely be a good thing.

The Rearview Mirror

It's been quite a few years since my first RV park purchase, and I can proudly say I have learned a lot about operating an RV park. (My children and I are also healthy and happy, despite my various activities while pregnant.)

I turned the property into a short-term rental park and made dozens of changes and upgrades. I built up enough equity in the property to leverage it and purchase additional properties. I now own many RV parks, mobile home parks, multifamily units, and a boutique motel. All my properties are self-managed, and I was able to do all of that without any investors or private equity.

Looking back, I'm often reminded of one of my influencers, Sam Zell, a billionaire real estate investor and philanthropist, who once said, "I was successful because I didn't know I shouldn't have been." That describes my start in real estate. I shouldn't have asked for the loan. I shouldn't have been given the loan. If you consider what I know now compared to how little I knew at 26 years old, it's remarkable that I made it through the learning curve. I wasn't qualified. I knew nothing about the industry. I had no one to mentor me (or tell me how little I knew).

But there's one thing I want you to take from my start in RV park investing: You don't need to know everything about a potential investment to be successful. Sometimes, you just need to act. If you have others who can be a resource (like I hope to be for you), then by all means, lean on them. Learn what you can, but also take action. You'll be glad you said yes now instead of letting it become "I should have" in the rearview mirror.

Don't Forget the Why

Finally, don't forget why you are doing this. And I hope it's not just to get rich. (I assure you, that won't bring you the happiness you think it will.)

As I said earlier, I sought the freedom and flexibility to spend time with my family. I knew I wanted to model a relationship with work that allowed my children to feel important. I wanted my kids to see me build something and do it while being present in their lives.

While I was chasing this dream, I also learned that I really enjoy serving people. I have beautiful memories of people having some of the greatest times of their lives at one of my parks. My guests experienced true happiness, and I was able to play a part in that.

I also love that you are reading this book, which can play a part in your path to freedom and flexibility. This is why I hold free seminars and mentor hundreds of people. I feel truly blessed to be able to help others—to bring happiness, success, or even just knowledge to people. Those are some of the greatest rewards and a big part of my "why."

We live in a world of abundance. There is plenty to go around. We don't need to keep success to ourselves. We don't need to hide the way we built something from others for fear that they might compete with us. Share yourself, and you will receive the greatest gift of all. Thank you for joining me on this journey.

THE WHY AND HOW OF PURCHASING RV PARKS

Chapter 1

RV CAMPING: THEN AND NOW
(AND WHY NOW IS A GREAT TIME TO INVEST)

America has always enticed exploration. From the time Native Americans spanned the continent to the time Europeans claimed it as their own, every culture has revered the opportunity to explore the varied expanse between the Atlantic and Pacific shores. We have learned about historic journeys across land, including the Lewis and Clark expedition and the Oregon Trail. Our minds have always been captivated with what is out there that we haven't yet seen before. Whether exploring by the shoes on our feet or covered wagon or automobile, adventure is a key element to our culture and soul.

It didn't take long after the first automobile made its appearance on U.S. roads in 1893 for Americans to start thinking about how they could put all of the comforts of home on four wheels. In 1904, the earliest known version of an RV was built—by hand—on top of an automobile chassis. It boasted two bunk beds, an icebox, incandescent lights, and a radio. It had just enough room for four people.

At the same time, camping was becoming increasingly popular, boosted by books and newspapers that offered pictures of previously unseen and amazing places. What started as backpacking became camping via horseback. Eventually, wagons and vehicles became the preferred methods to reach the great outdoors.

The Conklin Family Gypsy Van

In 1915, a New York bus manufacturer named Roland Conklin took recreational travel to an entirely new level when he unveiled his luxurious, eight-ton Conklin Family Gypsy Van. With an onboard hot-water shower, a covered observation deck, and a dance floor, Conklin took his family on a much-publicized trip across the country, starting in Albany, New York, and arriving in San Francisco, California, two months later.

The *New York Times* wrote articles about the family and their revolutionary new vehicle, and the Conklins made sure to stop for photo opportunities and chats with admirers throughout their journey. To Conklin's delight, onlookers were mesmerized by the twenty-five-foot, double-decker minibus. Conklin proudly showed off how a family could live aboard for extensive trips, given the early RV's kitchen, bathroom, and sofas that easily turned into beds. Such a fully equipped vehicle opened up a world of possibilities for those who wanted to explore faraway places but not be confined to the schedule and stops of a train. The desire for a home on wheels—one that you could take almost anywhere—was born.

The Model T and the Original Traveling Groups

In the early 1920s, Henry Ford offered a specialized version of the Model T that satisfied the desire for a motorized home that people could live in for extended trips. Owners of these vehicles formed traveling groups, and the term "tin can tourists" took hold. Famous for eating most of their meals out of tin cans, the community grew to nearly 300,000 drivers and even adopted a special pin so they could easily spot fellow members along their journeys.

In the late 1920s, the Great Depression hit the U.S., and living on the road became the only option for a lot of families. Even though the trend of living on the road full time started out of necessity, many people grew accustomed to this nomadic lifestyle and continued it even after the economy bounced back.

Enter the Trailer

Since the special Ford Model Ts were clunky and expensive, competitors soon developed alternative models. Trailers became more popular, as they could be towed and left at campgrounds. This allowed trailer owners who were seeking work to drive their vehicle around without dragging the entire family with them.

The trailers also became more comfort focused and began to shift away from the boxy profile of early RVs. In 1934, the first aerodynamic trailer, known as an Airstream, came on the market. Inspired by the aircraft of the day, the curved aluminum exterior minimized wind resistance, improved durability, and decreased the weight of the trailer. An enclosed galley kitchen, onboard water supply, and electric lights allowed families to live in unprecedented comfort. Despite the high cost of $1,200 (more than most families made in a year at that time), Airstream's first model, the Clipper, flew out the doors.

Demand Goes up and Supply . . . Closes Up?

Trailer sales boomed, and more companies started manufacturing fancier trailers and RVs, but no one predicted what would happen next. On December 7, 1941, the Japanese attacked Hawaii's Pearl Harbor, and the U.S. entered World War II. Leisure travel and the materials needed to build trailers were luxuries the U.S. could no longer afford. Structural aluminum became classified as a critical war material, available only for the building of vital aircraft. Tires and gasoline also became scarce, and Airstream had no choice but to close its doors.

Fortunately, with the end of the war, the pent-up demand and desire to forget some of the atrocities of war prompted Airstream and other RV manufacturers to reopen, and the U.S. entered a new era of recreational travel. Led by veterans reunited with their families, sales began to sky-rocket, and additional competitors entered the market.

RVs through the Decades

In the 1950s, companies like Winnebago introduced customizable RVs through do-it-yourself kits. The new RVs also had plumbing systems, making traveling a breeze compared to that with older trailers. When the 1970s hit, young people were looking for affordable ways to travel between music festivals and political protests, and the appeal of RVs rose yet again.

Over the next couple of decades, manufacturers found ways to make RVs cheaper. Many manufacturers (not including Airstream) replaced aluminum with less expensive materials. Vehicles became more affordable, durable, and larger over time.

By the early 2000s, the variety of trailers and RVs was so vast that families of any size could find an RV to fit their needs. On the high end, Airstream continued to buck the trend of becoming cheaper and bigger by consistently producing new, unique models coated entirely in aluminum. Motor coach manufacturers also launched lines so luxurious that headliner bands preferred them over other modes of transportation. Some models offered over 350 sq. ft. of space (the size of an apartment in some cities), and prices could easily exceed six figures.

On the other end of the spectrum, simple, fully functional RVs cost less than the price of some cars. For the first time ever, young adults could afford months-long adventures and even work as they traveled the country. When they finished that stage of their lives, they still had the underlying investment—the RV or van—that they could sell and use the proceeds to start their next stage.

With the advent of social media, movements like #RoadLife and #VanLife have prompted people to explore the world via RV travel, or watch those who do with envy through their phones.

Today, RV customizations are limitless. Want a special compartment so you can travel with your favorite lizard? Totally doable. Need solar panels so you can live off the grid? Check.

RV Parks Are Reaping the Benefits

With the arrival of COVID-19, in 2020, it was no surprise that the popularity of RVs reached its highest point ever. Faced with the alternative of staying at home with restricted social gatherings, the prospect of taking to the road sounded better than ever during the pandemic. For those who didn't venture out, the pent-up wanderlust has driven them to new travels now that the danger has ebbed.

Every age group has a reason to choose RV life over any other form of travel. For retirees, RV life offers a safe, inexpensive way to see all their favorite locales or their bucket list travel destinations. For midlifers who are starting to question the purpose of life and their work/life balance, RVs offer an opportunity to obtain some balance while still having office space when needed. Now that many people work remotely, rather than going into an office, remote work from an RV is more attractive than ever.

And finally, for twenty-somethings who are just starting their careers, the global pandemic provided many with a feeling of uncertainty. As a result, this generation believes that if you want to do something extraordinary, now is the time to do it. You can't wait to start exploring, because nothing about the future is certain. The RV lifestyle appeals to the digital generation, who can take their work with them and see the world.

These Aren't Your Grandparents' RV Parks

Modern RV parks offer themes and amenities that never existed decades ago. Whether you are looking to get deep off the grid and enjoy time in nature or you want to golf, soak in a hot tub, and visit upscale restaurants, today's RV parks offer a wide array of options.

There are also communities of RV parks all over the country. The U.S. has over 13,000 private RV parks and 1,600 state parks with spots for campers. Gone are the days of feeling alone as you travel. RV travelers have started to network with like-minded campers, and building kinship is easier than ever. Some travelers plan years in advance, booking their favorite spots next to their favorite traveling friends.

One of my modern parks featuring high-end amenities.

The world of RV parks is only getting bigger and better. What was once regarded as just a road trip has become a lifestyle choice—a choice of freedom, a choice to not live in a single place for years at a time, and a choice to see the treasures of our continent. RV park perks just keep getting better, which makes every new year all the more exciting.

This is why the present offers the best opportunity ever to capitalize on the demand for the RV lifestyle. For decades, our culture has valued the ability to travel and explore our vast continent. And that desire to explore has exploded—with more enticing options than anyone could have imagined. I encourage you to continue reading, and explore how you can join in this adventure. If your experience is anything like mine, I know you will enjoy the ride.

Chapter 2

DIFFERENT PARKS FOR DIFFERENT FOLKS

As you begin to think about investing in an RV park or campground, you need to consider the type of park you are hoping to purchase. Just as there are different RVs for the many types of people, there are also varying types of RV parks. And I embrace that variety. Are you looking to go far away from civilization and enjoy the beauty that only nature can offer? There are gorgeous RV parks for you. Likewise, if you are looking for amenities and activities that rival a five-star hotel, you can find parks that deliver just such an experience. Let's go over some of the most common RV park categories. We'll get into detail about accommodations and amenities in Part 2, so for now, let's start to build your search criteria as you begin to think about investing in an RV park.

Mobile Home Parks

First, let's clear up a common misunderstanding. The terms "RV parks" and "mobile home parks" are often used interchangeably. The truth is that they are very different. At the core of their differences is the length of stay.

At RV parks, people tend to come and go as they please, much like a hotel or campground. In mobile home parks, people often stay for years, and these tenants pay rent each month for the right to keep their mobile home on a lot. The term "mobile home" is somewhat of a misnomer as most owners never move their home once they place it on a lot. If a family wants to move or upgrade, they often sell the mobile home in its lot and find a new one somewhere else, because it can cost thousands of dollars to move a mobile home.

Mobile home parks are also distinguished by the way utilities are divided. It is common for mobile home park residents to pay for individually metered utilities like water and sewer in addition to their rent payments, much like tenants do in homes and apartments. This is advantageous because it invalidates any suggestion that utilities are unfairly divided. As with condos and apartments, a mobile home park can evict a tenant if they don't pay the rent for their lot.

RV Parks, in Contrast

RV park residents are transient, so these parks typically charge for short-term stays with daily, weekly, monthly, or seasonal fees for visitors to keep their space. Each park has its own policy on how long you can stay.

The rules of some short-term parks impose length-of-stay limits between seven and thirty days. Unlike a mobile home park, the cost of water and sewage is often included in the RV park fee. These visitors expect to pay higher fees per day for the convenience of coming and going.

I should also point out that RV parks aren't associated with the typical mobile home park stigma, which tends to be thought of as a burden on the community and a low-income neighborhood with the associated problems of drugs and crime. Because RV parks typically attract a higher-income demographic, local boards are much more friendly to zoning approvals. In recent years, many cities and towns have been reluctant to allow the development of new mobile home parks. At best, they allow existing mobile home parks to be grandfathered in. But RV parks are often viewed very differently and don't face these same issues in most locales.

Another major distinction between mobile home parks and RV parks is rent control. This is highly dependent on local regulations, but RV parks are generally exempt from rent control ordinances, while mobile home parks tend to be subject to them.

It is imperative that you do your research when considering a purchase with these differences in mind. A major benefit of an RV park over a mobile home park is the potential for financial growth. RV parks are commercial properties that can increase in value significantly. They also tend to create a significant return on investment (ROI) compared to mobile home parks. But rent control regulations can severely hamper your ROI if they apply to your park.

Another consideration is that RV parks are trending in popularity; mobile home parks are not seeing the same excitement. In 2021, there were over 13,000 RV businesses across the nation with a total annual revenue of $38 billion.[1] This number is growing exponentially, with the current rate of growth exceeding 13 percent year over year.[2]

Types of RV Parks

Before we get into the details, let's discuss the types of parks that exist out there. It's important to understand them, as each one has characteristics that are important to both RV park owners and guests.

The Competition: Government Lands

Some of the most beautiful places in our country are found in national and state parks. It's not surprising that these parks are destinations for millions of RV enthusiasts each year, as campers tend to enjoy the outdoors. But the government parks typically offer rustic accommodations. They may not accommodate large campers (sometimes they permit only tent camping), and it is rare that a government-run campground has many amenities. Sometimes, they even offer limited or no hookups for water, sewer, or electric. This makes a long-term stay nearly impossible, and it greatly limits the type of camper who will choose to stay in the park.

You can't buy an RV park to run inside a state or national park, but if you understand the competition that the government campground offers, you can better position your own nearby investment. Learn how nearby attractions and parks operate and what they offer so you can differentiate yourself. Market your park to those who look for accommodations that can't be found on government land.

---

1   Kampgrounds of America Research, *North American Camping & Hospitality Report*, 2023, http://koa.uberflip.com/i/1497941-2023-north-american-camping-outdoor-hospitality-report/0?.

2   Kampgrounds, *North American Camping*.

Long-Term Parks: Monthly and Seasonal

Long-term parks are great investments that operate similarly to a mobile home park or an apartment complex. Guests pay rent—typically on a monthly or a seasonal basis—and may even enter a lease with the park owner. The parks tend to bill for utilities like electricity and water, and tenants tend to stay for months, if not entire seasons. The amenities found at long-term parks also vary dramatically, from almost no amenities to properties that offer laundry services and gyms for their tenants.

From an investor's perspective, long-term parks are advantageous for two main reasons. First, they are less intensive to manage and could be run by a management company. By using a management company, your park could truly be a passive investment. (If you are unable to find a management company, try looking into companies that manage mobile home parks in the area. The responsibilities are essentially the same.) Second, long-term parks that have fewer amenities will have fewer capital expenses. Fewer capital expenses mean fewer surprises and a smaller, more stable operating budget.

At a seasonal park, tenants pay rent for the entire season. These destinations typically experience ideal weather during a certain part of the year and are less popular during the offseason. For example, Florida has a large share of seasonal parks that are popular in the winter months, since the weather is more temperate and predictable during that time.

During offseasons, seasonal parks may close, but some will permit campers to leave their RVs on location, providing a storage service. Offering RV storage tends to have a secondary benefit: the return of the renter. Why drive to a new park when your RV is already at last year's park?

Short-Term Parks and Why I Love Them

My favorite type of investment property is short-term parks because of the sheer number of ways you can improve them and make them stand out. Let's dive in and discuss why these top my list.

For an RV traveler who's looking to stay somewhere for a short time—from a single night to a few weeks—there are three different types of short-term parks. The first type is the RV park equivalent of a roadside motel. Guests tend to be traveling to a different destination and are merely looking for an overnight stay before getting back on the road in the morning. These are typically found a short distance from an interstate highway or heavily traveled corridor.

The second type of short-term park is more like a hotel. Travelers seek out these parks for longer stays, typically because they are in the area for a purpose. It could be that their family lives nearby, or perhaps there is a concert, sporting event, or conference in town. Sometimes, the park is located near a larger city that is a tourist destination.

The average stay at these types of parks is usually two or three days. These parks tend to have more amenities available, such as a check-in office, a swimming pool, a laundry room, and/or a dog park.

One of my camp stores.

The third type of short-term park is more like a destination resort. In the case of RV parks, part of the resort's hospitality is the outdoors. Guests stay at these properties for a few days to a few weeks. Often, these parks *are* the destination, and people reserve them months in advance to get the resort with the location, view, and amenities they want.

The goal of this property type is to capture guests' full attention and keep them in the park for the entire vacation. Similar to high-end destinations like Disney World, these parks house their guests, feed them, and entertain them, so there is no reason to leave. These resorts can have such a wide range of amenities that it's exciting to think of the possibilities. I've seen wagon rides, fine dining, laser tag, water parks, theatrical performances, and full activity schedules at these destination-style parks. They also earn the right to charge more, since the amenities and entertainment can save the guests the expense and hassle of traveling elsewhere for amusement. Revenue-generating side hustles are limited only by your imagination. Of course, these properties are heavy on operational needs. We will cover how to explore and plan for those needs in Section 3.

Combination Parks

Yet another RV park option blends the features of a long-term park and a short-term park. These combination parks have separate areas for short- and long-term visitors. The theory is long-term residents don't want to be placed next to a group having a fireside party during their short-term stay. Likewise, the short-term visitors would likely rather interact with others who are traveling. Separating the guests in a combination park keeps each type of RV owner as comfortable as possible.

Another variation of a combination park is one that houses RVs and mobile homes. These are typically long-term parks, with long-term RV campers in one section and mobile homes in another.

Man Camps

I hesitate to use this term, since "man camps" are not exclusively for men. But historically, you would find mostly men at these properties, which is how they earned the name.

Man camps typically consist of workers staying in a certain area for a few months or a year while they're working on a job site. For example, they could be building a factory or a pipeline, and the camps offer an affordable housing option that keeps everyone near the construction site. Workers frequently travel from far away for the opportunity to perform this temporary but lucrative work. In some long-stay situations, entire families live in the camps.

Man camps have been around for centuries, dating back to the 1800s in the United States. Today, they tend to be popular during oil booms and gold rushes, in places like Texas and North Dakota. They are also commonly used by installation crews at solar panel and wind turbine locations.

Man camps tend to be good options for long-term projects like these because they are much cheaper than hotels and typically offer full hook-ups. They also provide flexibility since workers can extend their stay if the job takes longer than planned.

From an investor's standpoint, it is important to do a full evaluation before purchasing a park for this clientele since these parks bear different risks than other types of RV parks. Some of the crucial information unique to man camps includes the expected longevity of employee stays, the stability of the project, and whether and when project hiring will increase or decrease. Due to these variables, it is very difficult to evaluate this type of property.

Specialty RV Parks

Specialty RV parks are another niche investment, but they may be attractive for park owners looking to be part of a unique, tight-knit community. Specialty parks cover a wide range of variations but usually cater to a subset of people looking to stay with like-minded guests. Specialty parks may come with a premium, but if the parks perfectly cater to the clientele's desires, they are highly sought after.

Age-Restricted Parks

One example of a specialty park is one that only allows guests over 55, also known as an age-restricted park. As you'd expect, these parks are found in popular retirement locations such as Florida and Arizona and cater to active, retired guests who would rather not worry about noisy neighbors and young children running around. (Some may allow temporary stays by younger visitors, as long as they are sponsored by a guest.) The parks may include golf courses, pools, restaurants, and many amenities found in retirement homes. Social activities abound, with organized games, potlucks, craft-making sessions, and live music festivities packed into most weeks.

RV-Restricted Parks

Another type of specialty park restricts the type of RV allowed. For example, some parks only allow guests with RVs that are no older than ten years; this restriction is particularly common in Florida and Arizona. Other parks restrict guests to only those with Class A motorhomes (those that are built on a truck or bus chassis)—effectively weeding out newbies and those who can't afford the largest class of motorhome.

Clothing-Restricted Parks

There are also specialty parks for people who really want to become one with nature. With dozens of nudist RV parks in the United States and counting, this is an increasingly popular type of specialty park. Many of the nudist parks are in Florida (the beautiful beaches and warm weather likely play a role). After all, aside from a few days a year, most people would not consider Alaska the ideal place to run around naked.

Naturists who stay at these specialty parks may sunbathe, take walks, and swim in the nude. Owners of nudist RV parks take extra precautions to protect the privacy of their guests. All visitors usually undergo a background check before they arrive. Photography is not permitted on these sites. Owners also strategize to ensure that they have an approximately even number of male and female guests at the park.

Inclusive Parks

You may be thinking, *But wait! Maybe guests want to hang out with the same sex!* Fortunately, there are parks for those folks as well. LGBTQ+ parks exist all over North America, from Canada to Palm Springs to Minnesota. They offer an inclusive environment for people of all sexual and gender identities. Many of these RV parks offer themes for their guests. The parks have outdoor movie nights, game nights, and dances. They cater to a wide variety of interests, with some guests staying just for a weekend getaway, and some for months. There is always some kind of exciting event going on at LGBTQ+ specialty parks.

An RV Park for Everyone

As this chapter suggests, RV parks come in just about every flavor that we humans can dream up. And I love that about RV parks.

In this asset class, your income is only limited by your imagination. Perhaps as a kid, you always dreamed of going to a destination that had everything. Why not create it and have others pay you to visit? Or maybe you have always felt constrained by the reminders of human intervention at every corner of every street; your soul is most free when you are far from civilization. Well, there's an RV park with your name on it, and I'll be coming to visit.

I'll get into far more detail in the coming chapters about the many things you can do to make your RV park the ultimate destination, but hopefully this chapter has started to get the creative juices flowing.

RV parks can run the gamut from $30 per night to hundreds of dollars per night. Amenities can be nonexistent or extravagant. Your view could be highway lights, awe-inspiring mountain peaks, or dreamy sunsets on the beach.

The decision you now get to make is what kind of investment you want to own. If you do it right, it will make money. And even if you make some mistakes along the way (I certainly did), you can *still* make money.

Your RV Park Reflects You

Your RV park is the intersection of your journey as a creator, a host, an investor, as well as the various journeys of all the guests visiting your park. What will you do with that opportunity? That's where the fun begins. And it's also where your personality can make all the difference.

I believe the concept of "who, not how" applies to almost all the challenges you will experience with RV park investing. (If you haven't read Dan Sullivan's book by that title, I highly recommend checking it out.) How will you express your personality in the park? Who will you choose to manage the park, and what attributes will you look for in that person? You have the opportunity to design your park in a way that is unique and offers guests an elevated experience. Start to conceptualize your park with those guests in mind! Be exactly what they are looking for!

Chapter 3

EMBRACING THE CHALLENGES OF INVESTING IN RV PARKS

L et's get this out of the way up front: RV park investing is challenging. I believe the challenges are easily outweighed by the joys and benefits of owning an RV park, or I wouldn't be writing this. But let's just make it clear from the beginning—this investment class has its fair share of challenges. And I've learned to embrace them.

Investing in an RV park will be different from other investment classes you've previously considered. Even if you've invested in real estate before, you may be surprised by what it takes to invest in a park. It can be simultaneously draining (physically and emotionally) and a beautiful experience you will never regret.

We'll go into depth on how to overcome these investing headwinds in Part 3, but it's important for you to know what you're up against before you begin searching for your RV park.

Seasonal Challenges

RV parks often have challenges related to the change in seasons. Perhaps it's the weather, or a seasonal venue that your park adjoins. But the fact that RV parks frequently have fluctuating business is one of the largest challenges of all.

In some extreme examples, like Florida and Arizona, parks may witness full-capacity bookings through the entirety of winter, while summers may see occupancy rates drop to single digits. First, let's take a moment to be thankful. If you own a park with such a seasonal swing, you have an opportunity to max out your capacity for a significant portion of the year. That likely means you have additional opportunities to increase revenue. Consider this challenge an opportunity in disguise.

As desirable as a place may be during some times of the year, there are others during which you will need to weather the bad weather. This is where your positivity and ingenuity can make all the difference.

Be Creative

Can you offer to store RVs at your location during your offseason? If so, you will increase your revenue, and you will increase the chance your guests come back to your park. If you stay open all year, you can store the RVs in a distant corner of the property, with zero impact to ongoing operations.

If you aren't open all year, what else can you do to monetize your property? Are there other businesses that close for the season? If so, you can offer storage for their vehicles (think boats, food trucks, or delivery vans). Again, your income is limited only by your creativity.

Be Prepared

I encourage you to prepare for slow times while the earnings are good. Review your annual and seasonal budgets carefully, and obtain a credit line for unexpected circumstances. Build in the cost of emergencies, and be prepared to act quickly if a once-in-a-lifetime occurrence—like COVID-19—comes out of nowhere.

As a business owner who stood to be incredibly impacted by COVID, I can attest that prompt action can be critical to saving your investments. Just about every business was impacted by COVID, and travel and leisure felt the brunt of the impact. When I saw closures happening, I called the bank immediately. I knew I wouldn't be able to evict people from my park for not paying rent, yet I also knew restrictions would greatly limit travel. I was heading for trouble.

Because I acted quickly, my bank gave me a large line of credit for my short-term properties, which were most at risk. The bank also offered to convert all my debt to interest-only for six months. This put me in a position to weather out the worst of storm. I know many other businesses were not so lucky.

Fortunately for my industry, the fear of COVID fueled the RV park business, and I didn't need to rely on my bank's offerings. But the best thing I did was work out arrangements with the bank before I needed to. Had I waited for a more critical stage, my chances of success would have diminished.

I'll also take this opportunity to plug the numerous advantages that exist when working with local banks. In business, relationships are everything, and in my experience, nationwide banks don't provide the flexibility that small, local ones do. Here's a good litmus test for which banks deserve your business: How often can you get a key decision-maker on the phone? I suspect you will find that local banks will be the most responsive and go out of their way to earn your business.

Operational Challenges

Seasonal parks require seasonal employees. Also, to operate a short-term RV park successfully, you'll need a much larger team than you would for a long-term park, multifamily property, or mobile home park.

Seasonal parks are far more labor intensive when it comes to operations. The owners of mobile home parks and multifamily properties typically only communicate with their guests to collect rent and take care of maintenance requests. By contrast, owners of RV parks and seasonal properties have daily contact with guests, and the in-park amenities frequently require additional maintenance.

The day-to-day operations of RV parks have many moving parts that must work together. Management helps new guests navigate the park and takes care of the park's various amenities. Everything must be in working order, from the laundry machines to the electricity, or the management will be responsible for the inadequacies. As more money-making amenities are added to the park, the responsibilities and the team must grow accordingly.

RV parks should ideally have someone available for guests 24/7, just in case an issue arises. Whether it's a problem with a certain guest's RV or with the property as a whole, a team member who knows the ins and outs of the RV park must be available to solve the problems that come up. And they will.

Issues like these can be contracted out on an as-needed basis, but you will pay a premium for late-night visits to the park, assuming you can find someone available. Moreover, attempting to hire out everything will impact your profits. You are essentially training and accompanying every serviceperson who comes into your park. I have found it is far more effective to have an on-site maintenance person. Some of my most knowledgeable on-site employees have been living at the park for years, and they approach their work as if it were on their own house. Not only are they available at a moment's notice, but they also have intimate knowledge of how things work because they spend all day and all night there.

Managerial Challenges

Delegating tasks to others comes with a learning curve. The park's owner and/or manager must learn to assign various tasks to other employees, so the park stays clean and intact. Decisions as to who receives delegated tasks should incorporate not only who possesses the skills for the job, but also who excels in guest interactions.

Operating an RV park has many outwardly visible tasks, offering managers and employees frequent opportunities to interact with guests. As an investor, it is important to find employees who deliver top-notch customer service at every opportunity. In my early years of park ownership, I was on the premises daily; I even lived in the park for a period of time. This gave me invaluable insights as to how significantly an employee could impact my guests' happiness.

For the investor who wants a more hands-off approach, it's possible to hire a customer-focused manager and team. This what I do with most of my parks now, but I make sure it's easy to receive feedback from our guests, so I know how things are going. I seek feedback in numerous ways, including customer surveys (digital and paper), online reviews, and software platform reviews.

The Significance of Skill Sets

The on-site manager or owner should have a broad skill set (or develop one), unless the team already has numerous skill sets covered. RV parks can have issues ranging from electrical to plumbing to housekeeping to computer networking, and the best management team has each type of issue covered by at least one team member. If the management team is one person, it is imperative that person is a jack/jill-of-all-trades or is willing to learn quickly.

The Importance of Time and Physical Energy

The management team also needs to spend a lot of time at the property—including holidays and weekends, since that's when most people take vacations.

There are ways to make this enjoyable, and if you make it fun for the staff, that spirit will spill over to the guests. I have spent many Thanksgivings making turkeys for hundreds of people, as well as Easters putting on egg hunts, reading stories, and serving food to all the families in the park. Owners who choose to run the business by themselves should expect not only to invest money but also significant time at the park if they want to make a profit.

I often hear "I would love to own an RV park when I retire." Many people realize that running an RV park requires a lot of time, and retirees have plenty of this resource. However, let me dispel this myth for you: Even if you have a lot of time on your hands, this is not a retirement job unless you have loads of physical stamina. Most people want to start relaxing as they head into their sixties, and owning and operating an RV park requires significant energy.

Marketing Challenges

If you want guests to stay at your campground, they must be able to find it easily. Gone are the days of people locating you via a road atlas or telephone book. Campers now rely on apps and Google searches to see what options are available. Creating a Google business page and social media accounts are a must for your RV park, as is getting listed on various camping apps.

Once you have a digital presence, you need to maximize that presence. The best way to do that is get reviews from guests to show why you stand out from the next RV park. Reviews help you grow organically, while simultaneously boosting your visibility with Google and other search engines. If you can collect hundreds or thousands of five-star reviews, your park will be a top contender. Oftentimes, reviews alone will sell a customer on your property. This further underscores why your customer service is of utmost importance at your park. You want to wow people so much that they can't imagine giving you less than five stars in a review; ask them on the way out to do so.

The Challenges of DIY

When you manage the park yourself, it's very difficult not to spend all your time wrapped up in the day-to-day tasks of running the place. To this day, I still get sucked into day-to-day operations like taking reservations or making pizza when I'm on-site at a park. But only I can work on the overall strategy and growth of my business; no one else can do that for me. My manager can take reservations, and my staff members can make pizza. Spending too much time working *in* the business but not *on* the business is a dangerous path that I encourage you to depart from as soon as possible.

A few years ago, I decided to move to a different state than where my entire portfolio was located. Since I did, my focus has shifted away from going on-site to solve the problem du jour and toward long-term growth and strategies. And do you know what happened? My net worth has more than doubled since my move.

Admittedly, I had some rock stars to thank for a lot of that growth, but by not being there, I enabled them to step up to the plate. I'm with Tim Ferriss (author of *The 4-Hour Workweek*) on this one: If you enable your employees to make decisions for you up to a certain, agreed-upon point, you are trusting them more, allowing them to grow more as leaders and ultimately saving yourself from day after day of inefficiency.

Employees who feel trusted will care more about the park and believe their decisions make a difference in how well the park is run. That will trickle down to how guests feel when they interact with your frontline employees.

For Every Season

Now that you've delegated responsibilities and given employees ownership in some decisions, you have time to create the two different plans you need for seasonal RV parks: an offseason schedule and a peak-season schedule.

Your offseason schedule should consist primarily of the tasks that would cost you dearly if performed during peak season. This includes any project that would shut down an area of your park or affect your income stream. For example, I own a glamping (glamorous camping) facility that I wanted to repave. It wasn't an emergency, but since the aura of glamping requires keeping an entryway that feels upscale, I wanted to schedule it. My contractors told me it would take three days, and the entire park would be inaccessible during that time. I would have sacrificed thousands of dollars in revenue if I had done it while the park was in season, so I scheduled the project for the offseason to make sure that business wasn't interrupted.

The same philosophy applies to housekeeping. During peak season, housekeepers have plenty to do to turn over the rental units between guests. During the offseason, I tend to keep them full time so that they can deep clean every inch of the property, getting it ready for the high traffic that will soon return. (Of course, this decision depends on how long your offseason is and where your park is located.)

Emergencies sometimes happen, but you can minimize them by keeping up with your maintenance and capital expenses, while inconveniencing your guests as little as possible. Leave minor projects for the peak season, such as mulching your grounds, planting new flowers, adding gravel where needed, or maintaining low-traffic areas. Schedule your major projects for the offseason, so you won't impact your revenue stream and your employees can help out because they aren't as busy with guest duties.

Final Thoughts

Like with any business, there will be challenges when it comes to investing in an RV park. You'll make mistakes. There will be a learning curve. And you will need to develop the skills and knowledge to really understand how the industry works.

Some of these things are out of your control as an investor, which is why it's so important to devote time to the parts of your business that you can control: keeping your park clean, treating your team extremely well, and making sure you have a preventive maintenance plan. With some forethought and planning, you can keep problems and headaches to a minimum and enjoy the fruits of your investment of time and money.

Chapter 4

SEARCHING FOR RV PARK OPPORTUNITIES

Perhaps the most common question I am asked is how to find RV parks and campgrounds that are for sale. Most people know about the MLS (Multiple Listing Service), but RV parks can't be found there. RV parks and campgrounds generally fly under the radar far more than most commercial real estate properties.

Before starting my foray into RV park ownership, I was a broker at the fourth-largest commercial real estate firm in the world. During my time there, I participated in over $300 million of RV and mobile home park transactions. I learned firsthand that certain methods of locating these hard-to-find assets worked better than others.

Finding by Knowing

The first step to finding a great deal on an RV park is to know what you're looking for. The following questions are particularly helpful in narrowing your focus:

- What parts of the country are attractive to you?
- What are your investment goals? Is this investment going to be passive, or do you want to be heavily involved?

- Are you looking for a certain type of park? Consider the types we covered in Chapter 2 and which ones appeal to you.
- What is your ideal price point?
- Which amenities would be most attractive to your guests?
- Are you looking for something that has opportunities to build upon, or would you prefer a park that is already there?
- What's your exit strategy? Are you planning to build this into additional investments down the road? Or is this just a single investment that you plan to build and improve, only to sell later?

Thinking through your options and pinpointing what you want in an RV park will save you time and help focus your search.

Location

Nearly everyone in residential real estate repeats the mantra, "location, location, location." This phrase is just as relevant to RV parks as well, but there's a nuance. Not only should you consider what areas of the country appeal to you, but you should also consider what regions will give you the best bang for your buck. Let's review the process of homing in on a location for your RV park investment.

Some investors look for an investment in a region that is appealing to them. Perhaps they have treasured memories from there, maybe they love the scenery, or it might just be they have family nearby. Other investors might get even more granular by specifying the exact city or county that they prefer. This could be because there is an attraction in the area, or it could be that the region has favorable laws or regulations. As I mentioned earlier, regulations can be severely impactful with mobile home park investments, but sometimes RV parks are impacted as well. In other words, think about what your goals are, and make sure your investment reflects those.

My first investment brought me familiarity, as it was in my home state. There's nothing wrong with buying something familiar, but there are several other factors to look for that are unique to RV park investments.

Accessible to Destinations

One of the biggest location factors is whether your park is easily accessible. This is part of making sure your investment dollars go a long way.

Are there major highways in the area? Are there tourist attractions nearby and within easy access of where you want to invest? If you are instead investing in a park that *is* the destination, such as a theme park or one that is far removed from civilization, you still need to consider how people will get to your park. "A thousand miles from nowhere" is going to be a hard sell for most RV travelers. Short-term parks especiallywill suffer from lack of access.

Your choice of location and its accessibility is critical for selecting an existing park or one you are looking to build. Spend a considerable amount of time thinking about this factor as your long-term success will be dependent upon it, and you can't change it later.

Accessible to Guests

There's a second part of accessibility that is also a critical consideration. You might be near highways or points of interest, but can you welcome large RVs, such as fifth wheels and Class A vehicles? When doing due diligence on potential investments, drive to the park from numerous access points to assess how easily your guests can get to your park. If it is difficult to get large vehicles into your campground, you've greatly limited your clientele, cutting off the wealthier end of the guest population spectrum. Even the positioning of trees and powerlines can impact potential patrons, and RVs tend to get bigger with time.

This second accessibility factor became even more personal to me recently when my kids and I took an extended road trip with a 25-foot camper in tow. I did the research ahead of time and planned visits to parks that accommodated our vehicle and camper. But as we approached one of the parks, I began to regret every mile. The road was dangerous for the size of trailer we were pulling, and by the time we arrived, I was completely rattled. Had I been towing a fifth wheel (like many of the customers I welcome to my own parks), there's no way we would have made it. Unfortunately, it didn't matter how amazing the park was or how well the staff took care of us. It's hard to write a five-star review for a park with a precarious entrance, and I won't be returning.

Before you purchase a park, do the drive. You need to understand what you are asking of your customers. There aren't many ways to overcome a dangerous or difficult point of access. You will lose customers, or worse—you may endanger them. Consider the accessibility factor as one of your highest priorities.

Investment Goals and Type of Park

The goals you have for your RV park investment are also critical to your search. Are you looking for a passive (less hands-on) investment? If so, you'll likely look for long-term parks that minimize your tenant turnover time period. Are you looking for something an active role in your investment (more hands-on) that allows you to work in a new lifestyle? Short-term parks will be your best option. I've invested in both types of properties, and they both have amazing opportunities in their own ways. However, they come with extreme differences and are best navigated with completely different skillsets.

Chapter 2 provided a detailed analysis of the many types of parks, and your best investment is one that resembles your personality. Do a personal assessment as to what would excite you the most. If you are not excited about your investment, you're looking in the wrong place for the wrong purchase.

Price

As is the case with nearly everything, your options are limited by the price you are willing to pay. With any investment, there are additional up-front costs that you need to consider outside of the sticker price. These include closing costs, holding costs, utility deposits that are due on day one, and payroll. I would encourage you to have access to at least six months of operational costs as well, since you may need to spend money before you are in the black financially.

We'll cover your financing options in greater detail in Chapter 8.

Investment Type

They are different ways to approach an investment—whether you're looking for a property that's ready to go as is or a property that needs some TLC to benefit park guests. Some common investment types include the BRRRR method,[3] completing a 1031 exchange, and completing a buy and hold. The investment type will determine the financing options available to you. We'll go into detail about financing in Chapter 8, but it's important to think ahead as you begin your search for a property. The investment type should be top of mind as you set up your search criteria.

---

3   You can purchase the BRRRR book by David Greene on www.biggerpockets.com/store.

BRRRR

The BRRRR method—buy, rehab, rent, refinance, repeat—is a well-known real investment strategy. Investors purchase properties that are undervalued or in need of repairs. They often purchase these properties for a low price and factor in the rehab costs. The investor takes on the challenges of fixing up a property, and then they refinance that property to extract the sweat equity. These properties often sell for more than the original purchase price. Using the additional funds gained from the sale of the property, investors repeat the process with a new property.

If you already own an investment property, you could rehab and/or refinance it to get a down payment for an RV park, then start the BRRRR chain reaction to grow a portfolio of parks. You can find more about the BRRRR method on the BiggerPockets website or BiggerPockets podcast.

1031 Exchange

Another common investment strategy among real estate investors is completing a 1031 exchange. Named for the section of the IRS code that governs it, a 1031 exchange happens when an investor sells one property, then directly reinvests the proceeds into the next to avoid capital gains taxes. The IRS grants a limited time window to do such an exchange—which as of this writing is forty-five days to identify the potential replacement properties and 180 days to complete the exchange. Investors must act within this time window or face strict tax penalties.

Buy and Hold

You might be entering an RV park investment without the immediate thought of selling the property. This could be a long-term investment for you, and your goal is to keep the property as long as possible. In this case, your investment method is a buy and hold. You have a long-term vision for the property, with no plans to sell in the near term. The primary benefit of the property is the regular cash flow and growing your equity.

Whatever your investment strategy, your price range impacts your potential investment opportunities, and any searches you perform should be influenced by how much you can invest to achieve the best return on your investment. There are lots of factors outside of price to consider when searching for properties (many of which are detailed in this book). It's important to consult with a skilled lawyer and accountant as you approach the purchase of an RV investment property.

Exit Strategy

The final step in any investment is the exit strategy. Regardless of when or how you plan to make your exit, you should consider this before you buy the property.

If you plan to hold the park in your portfolio for decades or pass the park down to your heirs, you will be less worried about your park appealing to buyers in the immediate future. However, if you plan to sell the park sooner rather than later, you should consider buying properties that are attractive to institutional investors.

Although real estate investment firms are starting to get involved in RV park investing, the industry hasn't consolidated around large players yet. We're seeing more and more institutions get in on the action—an assuring sign that it's a great idea to buy with an exit to the institutional investors in mind.

Institutional investors will more likely be interested in short-term parks that are in desirable locations near tourist towns or long-term parks in areas with large populations that show steady growth. They'll want a park with a minimum of 150 sites, with additional land to expand beyond 200 sites.

Even if your park has less than 150 sites, many institutional buyers like to see parks with room to expand. Because of this, buying a park with extra land will position you well when it's time to sell.

Ask questions to determine whether the land you're buying is developable. For example, I considered purchasing a tract of land that's attached to one of my short-term properties. Land has a longer due diligence period because you typically need to do more research than you would for residential real estate. When I was going through the due diligence process, I learned I would need $1 million in fill dirt just to get the land flat enough to develop the RV sites. That expense would push me well over $75,000 per site in development alone, which was way out of budget for that property and what I could charge for the sites there.

As you can see, there are a number of ways that things might not work out. Whether it's development costs or the regulations the city has in place for the land's use, make sure that the land you're buying can actually be used to make you money.

It is important to consider your goals as an investor as you begin your search for an investment property. By establishing your goals, price, location, investment type, and exit strategy, you're able to better prepare yourself for your investment. Being smart about how you will use the property now and in the future will help better shape your search and give you a better shot at investment success.

Chapter 5

FINDING RV PARK DEALS

A s I write this, real estate asset classes in the U.S. have witnessed several years of low inventory. It's caused prices to rise and investors to seek alternatives. RV park assets are certainly no exception.

Though the real estate market seems to be cooling down a bit at the time of this writing, RV parks continue to evade most investors. Let's talk about why that tends to happen and how it can be a good thing for a well-equipped, determined investor.

The Uniqueness of RV Parks

If you ask most people where to research properties for sale, they will send you to the MLS or a traditional real estate agent. What you won't usually find on the MLS or through a Realtor is an RV park. RV parks are considered commercial properties, and those are rarely listed on the MLS. Realtors who market and research commercial properties like RV parks are specialized. They aren't the typical agents you see hosting open houses on weekends.

The other uniquely challenging aspect of RV parks is that nearly 80 percent of the parks are owned by mom-and-pop businesses. These are often small, owner-operated RV parks. Sometimes these parks have been in the family for generations. This means you don't have a detached investor on the other end of the deal. Relationships matter. Your approach matters.

While the ubiquitous phrase "location, location, location" is certainly applicable in your RV park search, I'll add something to that: relationships, relationships, relationships. The following sections will help you understand how to locate RV parks for sale and build relationships with the potential sellers you find.

Cold-Calling

I know this might sound old school in these technology-driven days, but never underestimate the value of a pleasant voice on the phone. Given that many RV park owners are mom-and-pop, cold-calling can be a wonderful way to get in touch with the true decision-makers. Here are the steps I follow to make sure I reach the owners.

1. Create a list of parks that match your target profile. By now, you have thought about the type of park that fits your investment goals and your personality. (Read Chapter 2 again if you need help narrowing this down.)

2. Once you have your target profile, start looking at options. One of my favorite places to start my research is www.goodsam.com. Good Sam is a directory of RV parks across the U.S. and Canada, and it includes phone numbers, number of sites, existing amenities, and more for most parks. You may find that some of the information is outdated or incorrect, but in general, it's accurate enough to help you start cold-calling.

3. If you determine that a park is a good fit for you to buy, call the number and ask to speak with the owner. This is often the easiest first step you can take to sourcing deals in your RV park investment journey.

4. If you're unable to connect with the owner through the park's regular phone number, add it to a list of desirable parks and have the list skip traced. Skip tracing allows you to enter key data points, like the LLC that owns a park, and have the owner's name and number revealed. This allows you to call the owner directly without having to go through the park. Many skip tracing services exist, but be aware that the data from skip tracing isn't always as perfect as advertised. While I have used DealMachine for years, there are a number of good options to consider.

5. When you start hitting the phones, be sure to develop a rapport with the owners as quickly as possible. This will likely require an extra two minutes doing some research about the park, but these two minutes can go a long way. Rather than just calling and saying, "Hey, I want to buy your park," you can start with "I want to let you know that I love XYZ about your park so much that I'm interested in buying the place." You may be able to find some common ground with the owner and start building a relationship.

The key to cold-calling is to try to prolong the conversation as best you can and get as much information out of the owner in a way that's not intrusive. Try to identify pain points they may have, and be prepared to suggest how selling to you could alleviate that pain. At the end of the conversation, you want to position yourself as someone who the owner likes, remembers, and trusts. That way, when it does come time to sell, you're the first call they make.

Keep in mind that rejection is to be taken lightly. "No" usually just means "not right now," and buying an RV park is often a long game. I have had owners call me two years after my initial call, finally letting me know they were ready to sell. Had I taken that two-years-earlier no to heart or, God forbid, had I reacted negatively, I may never have had the opportunity to buy the place.

Keep things positive with the owners, and let them know that you'll welcome their call when the timing is better for them. Then make it a goal to maintain occasional communications with them so they remember you. Those communications take the form of a handwritten note, a Starbucks gift card, or whatever small token you can justify to let them know you're thinking about them. And most importantly, take great notes in your customer relationship management (CRM) tool so that you remember important details when the call does come.

Mail Outs

Just like with cold-calling, sending letters through the post office, also known as mail outs, can be an effective way to reach motivated sellers. Start with the Good Sam website to build your list of targeted parks.

One thing I encourage with mail outs is going the extra mile to find the actual owner names. Sending out generic, typed letters can look like a mass mailing, and addressing them to ABC Campground will result in a quick trip to the trash can. Remember—mailings are not as personal as a phone call, so it's important to up your game for mail outs.

I know this from experience on the receiving end. When one out of fifty mailings come addressed directly to me—perhaps even hand-written—I take notice. Even my staff takes notice, and they make sure I receive that mailing.

If your skip trace research provides a home address of the owners, I encourage you to use it. Now you have bypassed the chance that campground staff will get rid of your letter, and you will probably surprise and impress the owners by showing that you did your homework and found their home address.

Does this make you a stalker? I don't think so. It's just a friendly letter. Like with cold-calling, you want to stand out to the existing park owners as someone they will remember, like, and trust. This can be accomplished with a stamp and a thoughtful message. Something cold and generic like "we buy parks" probably won't capture an owner's interest. Instead, spend a few minutes finding some small details about the park's owners. You can look for information such as how long the park may have been in the family (something state records would reflect), or what some of the guests have said about the park and owners through reviews and social media accounts. Differentiate yourself from the competition. Add your own personal touch, and leave no room for the impression that this was a form letter sent out to thousands.

You can take another angle by personalizing the letter with your own details. For example: "My family is building its investment asset base so that we can one day bequeath it to our daughter" or maybe "We visited your park/the area and absolutely loved our experience." Your letter should articulate why you would be an attractive buyer. What can you do to make the seller's life easier and remove friction from the transaction? You should also mention your plans to continue the park's legacy of making it a top-notch experience for guests. I highly recommend combining cold-calling with a mail campaign for the most successful acquisition method.

The Overlooked Advantages of Direct Mail

You've probably received all sorts of mailings in your mailbox from Realtors, and you've probably wondered why they use direct mail so much. Most of those flyers live a quick life in someone's hands then land in the trash.

Direct mail is one of the most effective strategies in today's real estate investment landscape because it brings leads that are not already in the market. We call those "off-market" leads, rather than "on-market" leads through a broker. You can usually find better prices when you consider off-market leads.

Whether you create and mail letters yourself or use a third party to find these off-market leads, it's not as expensive as one might think. For example, I pay approximately $1 per letter, and I do six-month campaigns. Success rates vary, and one of the great things about direct mail is you only get warm leads. Interested sellers call *you*, which is different from cold-calling, door-knocking, or anything else.

It Stealthily Builds a Reputation

When a Realtor sends those shiny flyers to you over and over again, they are trying to build a relationship with you. Even though you may not reach out to them after the first, second, or even the tenth mailing, they know you will eventually remember their name. Their hope is when you need a Realtor, not only will their name be fresh in your mind, but their flyers will have already painted a professional image for you. This is precisely the first impression they want, and they got it for just a few dollars' worth of marketing materials.

Unlike most real estate agents, I don't send the same shiny flyer out repeatedly. I take a slightly different approach to optimize my direct mailings. I customize my message to cut through the noise of the rest of the marketing, which makes all the difference. RV park owners get plenty of solicitations and offers to sell their property. I look for ways to stand out by being more personalized; I prefer a warm encounter over a flashy flyer.

Repeat

Don't give up after a mailing or two. You haven't built your reputation yet. Since you saved yourself a few stamps by mailing only to the parks that you'd consider buying, persevere by doing consistent mailings every month or two for at least six mailings. Play the long game, especially with the bigger assets. You'll be surprised by who picks up the phone and calls when you least expect it, so review your list periodically so you don't get caught saying, "Who are you again?"

A few months ago, I was reminded of how powerful these direct marketing letters can be. One of the owners on my direct mail list called me after she had received a third letter from me. I consider a third letter to be early in the relationship.

This owner introduced herself by saying, "I don't have any intention of selling my building, but I'm just so amazed that you sent me three letters now, so I had to call and at least give you a brief opportunity to tell me what you're all about." This, my friends, is the definition of a "warm lead." By the end of the call, she had a sales price for me: "Well, admittedly, here's what my number would be."

That's the power of direct marketing. The relationship you build—even if it seems one-sided at first—carries so much more weight than most people realize. Once you build trust over the course of several months, people tend to let down their defenses. That relationship will frequently lead to a much better deal than had you been a stranger. Put yourself in the seller's shoes. Who would you feel more comfortable discussing your bottom line with—a total stranger, or someone who has taken the time to get to know you?

Stand out by Being Human, Not Commercial

I encourage you to distinguish yourself from the glossy flyers and commercial marketing pieces we all know so well.

How can you stand out? Handwrite your letter. Use a personally addressed, handwritten envelope because it says, "I took some time to send this, and this is of personal importance to me." Handwritten letters get opened nearly 100 percent of the time. You have the recipient's attention when they see their name inside. It may be the only personalized letter—with an authentic signature, no less—that they get that entire month. Make it something they will remember you by. You've now started that personal relationship.

Here are some other ideas to keep in mind with that personalized letter. Most likely, the owners you've identified in your short list are mom-and-pop operations. Maybe they've owned the park for decades; there might be a family story associated with it. They may have considered passing it on to their family, but for one reason or another, that's not the only option. They would also consider selling to someone they trust. This is where you come in.

Now that you've handwritten the envelope and signed your personalized letter, can you further your friendly, trustworthy relationship by including a photo? Absolutely! It's not a must, but I've done it with great success. You can include your kids in the picture, or even your favorite pet. The important thing here is letting the owner see the real person on the other end of the letter. This is not just an impersonal transaction—you are sharing your own family story as well.

With those personal touches, you start to create a picture in their heads, which is exactly what you want. Their park—what was once their baby—will be in the good hands of a caring new individual or family. When they pick up the phone to call you, the connection has already been formed in their heads. You couldn't ask for a warmer lead.

If you use a photo in the letter, consider using various occasions throughout the year as your excuse to follow up. For Thanksgiving, send well wishes from your family to theirs. Over the December holidays, include an updated photo with a quick note of how you are spending yours. When you give someone more than they would expect—when you are a friendly letter among hundreds of impersonal postcards and flyers—they will remember you. You've taken what's typically a chore for most people (opening the mail) and created an opportunity to connect. You've portrayed yourself as personable and authentic, and you've given the owner a pleasant picture of who's going to be on the other end of the phone when they give you a call.

Bring on the Talking Points

The professional relationship you've built also allows you to approach your talking points with more diplomacy. I frequently find that during due diligence, there's a factor (or several) about the park that may not be as perfect as it originally seemed. This can turn into an ugly sticking point if you don't have a relationship with the owners. But since they already regard you as trustworthy and professional, you can more easily approach a problem as just another factor in the negotiation process. These talking points allow you to lower your bid (often to a point where the park is an excellent deal) by identifying how these factors are opportunities for development. Emphasize that you want to alleviate those headaches for the owner, and you would be glad to take on the challenge for the appropriate price.

In one of my more stressful negotiations, a few weeks before closing, the bank decided they wanted 25 percent down instead of 20 percent. My cash was tapped out, as I was already paying almost $1 million down, and I didn't want to take on a partner.

So I renegotiated with the seller. Because of the relationship I had with him, he agreed to owner-finance the remaining 5 percent. I paid him monthly for three years in addition to the bank payments. That resolution was only possible because of the relationship I built during the due diligence process; he had originally said no to owner financing.

Keep things positive and diplomatic so that any snafus you run into will be minor bumps (rather than deal-breakers) with the backing of a long-standing professional relationship.

Niche-Specific Brokers

Another great way to find deals is through niche-specific real estate brokers. These agents specialize in just one or two asset classes. Getting deals through brokers is a great option because the experienced ones will be extremely familiar with the asset class and know exactly what to look for and what to avoid when it comes to buying an RV park. However, not all niche brokers are created equal. Do your due diligence before you trust their word. Just because someone is a niche real estate broker doesn't necessarily mean that they know RV parks. Find a broker that knows the types of parks you have chosen to pursue. You can find these professionals at large conferences or through a simple Google search.

People frequently ask me, "How can I be at the top of the broker's list when it comes time for them to sell a deal?" The answer is simple: Close on the deals that suit your criteria, and don't back out of offers. In other words, don't waste their time.

If a broker feels confident that you use their time wisely and close when you say you will, they will bring you deals, because that is how they get paid. For your part, don't make offers on deals you haven't already examined. There is nothing more frustrating for a broker than doing all the work for a property only to have a buyer get cold feet for no reason.

Of course, it's okay to back out if legitimate reasons came up during due diligence; that's exactly what due diligence is for. But when you start backing out or trying to renegotiate the price when it's not warranted, your likelihood of staying on that broker's short list will evaporate, and they might warn their broker friends as well.

When is a reason legitimate? Valid reasons for backing out of a deal usually include finding out the park has a significant flaw or negative factor that wasn't disclosed or that you weren't aware of before the due diligence period. Maybe it's a lawsuit against the park or an internal problem, like a tainted water supply. When the factor could greatly influence your return on investment or create a significant difference in the expenses or income you expected, that's a legitimate reason to back out or renegotiate.

The best thing you can do to keep deals coming from brokers is to keep this funnel open. Sign up for the appropriate niche-specific broker's and use their time wisely when a property you'd consider becomes available. Be straightforward and honest with your buying criteria. You are wasting the broker's time and yours if you ask them to send you properties you'd never consider or don't have the resources to purchase.

LoopNet and Crexi

When searching for deals, the final pipeline I'd recommend is commercial listing sites like LoopNet or Crexi. These sites are essentially the commercial real estate equivalent to the MLS. With both listing sites, you can create an account and narrow your searches so that only properties with your criteria are sent to your inbox. Sometimes, you will find that certain commercial brokers tend to specialize in the type of properties you are seeking. This is another way to find those niche-specific brokers. When you find them, get on their direct email list.

When reviewing deals on one of these sites, it's important to keep in mind that the numbers may be a bit inflated because the sellers are trying to attract a pool of buyers. But at the same time, there are deals to be had. Brokers sometimes pressure owners to lower prices since properties that stay on the list longer tend to lose buyers' interest. It's also not uncommon to find listings by owner.

Always request appropriate financial information on these documents, and go through them carefully during due diligence before making any purchase decisions. Brokers will often list projected numbers and price the deals accordingly. In most cases, I recommend using actual numbers instead of projected numbers. What did the park make last year? How much have the numbers gone up in the last five years? I trust actual numbers over projections every time.

Chapter 6
EVALUATING RV PARK DEALS

Once you have funneled some investment opportunities your way, it is critical that you have a consistent and reliable method of evaluating those opportunities. This section details the steps you should take when evaluating your investment options, including key indicators most investors look for in investment properties. I also review some of the most common mistakes that investors make.

Evaluating RV parks is more of an art than a science. While this chapter includes some of the metrics I look for when running my numbers, I can't emphasize enough that buying a property is not all about a cap rate (or rate of return). That's just one piece of the puzzle, along with some other standard metrics that you have probably seen used in other asset classes. When purchasing RV parks, however, the single most important metric is the profit and loss, or P&L. The "art" of this is the skill of being able to recognize when numbers look inflated, deflated, or just wrong. You need to develop the skill of recognizing when mom and pop have included their personal insurance or a personal vehicle for purposes of tax write-offs. These will not be required for *your* operation of the park and you have to take that into consideration.

I will point out that this is different from your typical single-family home investment. There is no black-and-white checklist that every park will be matched against. You have to get into the nuances of each park and how each owner has set up their P&L statements and tax write-offs.

As you review more and more parks, and continue on your path to purchasing a park, you will develop this art. And your questions for mom and pop will be paramount.

Get used to telling the owners "I am not the IRS. I'm looking for any expenses in here that were related to your personal expenses that may not transfer over to my costs of operation. Is your personal cell phone included in here? Your personal health insurance? Did you pay yourselves in payroll, or do I need to factor that in?"

If, as a potential investor, you only see $30,000 in payroll, but you see five people operating the park, you know someone was doing it without being paid or as an investor. Watch for those types of underestimated expenses, as you will have to hire someone to fill that role when you take over.

The lessons in this chapter are not always intuitive. Many of these concepts I learned after years of experience in the business and from listening intently to other savvy investors. If you keep an open mind and are willing to employ these techniques, I am comfortable saying you'll be in the best position to succeed in this industry.

My goal is to use this section to give you the tools and critical-thinking skills to decide which property is right for you. Each RV park has its own unique situation, and no two parks look or operate the same. That makes it challenging to figure out which parks stand out. Earmark this section as your go-to resource during your evaluation. If you have set up your business as outlined in the previous chapters, you will use this evaluation process frequently.

Existing Factors

A number of existing factors are important to your evaluation of whether a park is a good investment. The following includes a rundown of some the most critical factors.

Operating Costs (Profit and Loss Statements)

I never take the previous owner's summary of their operating costs as fact, and you shouldn't either. The absolute best way to understand a park's operating costs is to review three years' worth of profit and loss (P&L) statements. This shows the line-item expenses and income for the park and will give you a good idea of where the money is coming from and going to under the current management.

When picking apart the P&L statement, make sure the expenses are properly categorized. Make sure that everything on the P&L is truly a business expense. One common issue I've run into when reviewing a park's financial statements is that the owner may have many personal expenses included on the P&L. The owner is likely including personal expenses to reduce their taxable income. However, by having their own personal expenses shown on the P&L, the owner is actually doing themselves a disservice because they're reducing their net operating income (NOI). This is why I always tell people not to write off a deal based on the purported cap rate before reviewing the financial statements. The seller's cap rate might be lower than it will be when you're operating the park and doing the accounting properly.

Similarly, misallocated expenses can also change the cap rate and make a park look more attractive than it did originally. By combing through the P&L and other financial data, you can see if any expenses were excluded from the P&L, thus artificially inflating the cap rate. Not every mom-and-pop owner understands how to keep books. You need to understand the seller's financial data to get correct numbers around metrics like cap rates, spreads, and cash-on-cash returns, which we'll learn to calculate later in this chapter. You should also be thinking about additional nonnumerical factors that we discussed previously, like the number of sites, land for expansion, operational improvements, and deferred maintenance. While these factors aren't directly represented in a P&L or cap rate calculation, they can be the difference between a great deal and a lemon.

Park Ratings

One of the factors many people overlook when evaluating a park is its reputation, including its Good Sam rating. Whenever I evaluate a park, I check out its Good Sam ratings because Good Sam uses a well-known, unbiased system to evaluate parks.

Ratings can be useful when you're evaluating a park that you haven't yet visited in person. Good Sam rates RV parks with three numbers, on a scale of one to ten, for facilities, restrooms, and overall appeal. It's the most unbiased rating system for parks across North America that I've found because they utilize a standardized checklist for every property. I will say that there is some slight variation across the country because each territory or area has a different reviewer. So, what the reviewer in the Northeast might think is a great bathroom the reviewer in the Southeast might consider just average. Don't let the Good Sam ratings completely sway you, but know that it's one of the primary resources consumers use when they're considering a stay at your park.

I've also experienced the frustration of trying to achieve a perfect 10-10-10 rating, and I've learned not to hold it against parks that come close. I currently have a property that is rated a 10-10-9.5 park, and it generates great business. The 9.5 is based off one site on the whole property. Good Sam requires that each pedestal be thirty feet apart from the next pedestal. Unfortunately, I have a single pedestal that is twenty-nine feet apart from the next. My options are to redevelop the entire property to add an extra foot for that pedestal to get a perfect ten or leave the property as is. I can't justify the expense for a half-point point increase. But does it impress potential guests when your park is a perfect ten? You bet.

Evaluating Value

The current market value of the property is challenging to calculate with any certainty. A property is worth what someone is willing to pay for it, and that number changes all the time. If the market is hot, you may see sky-high asking prices. This is an important trend to consider since RV parks continue to increase in popularity as an investment for savvy businesspeople, both nationwide and globally.

No two parks are exactly alike, but there are a few calculations that can help you pinpoint exactly what an RV park is worth so you can get close to an apples-to-apples comparison of which investments are worth your time and money.

Cap Rate

A foundational piece of your investing journey is learning how to use a capitalization rate, more commonly shortened by investors to "cap rate." The cap rate is a metric of your rate of return on an investment. With commercial real estate, the cap rate is the most popular measure by which investments are assessed for profitability and return potential. Likewise, the cap rate is a helpful metric for an RV park investor, but it is certainly not the only thing to pay attention to.

The cap rate represents the yield of a property over a one-year time horizon and assumes the property is purchased in cash, not on a loan. (Cap rate calculations ignore costs associated with financing, like interest and closing costs, which can muddy the waters here.) In other words, if I purchased a property with cash, what rate of return would I have over a year, taking expenses into consideration but ignoring what a loan might cost?

To calculate the cap rate, divide a property's net operating income (NOI) by the current market value of the property. Your NOI is simply gross income minus operating expenses, which you should have from the P&L. If your gross income from your property is $1.1 million, and your operating expenses are $900,000, your NOI is $200,000.

Consider this hypothetical scenario:

Property Value	$2,000,000
Gross Income	$1,100,000
Operating Expenses	$900,000
Net Operating Income (Gross Income – Operating Expenses)	$200,000
Cap Rate (NOI ÷ Property Value) × 100	10 percent

A Note on Cap Rates

In general, the higher the cap rate, the more lucrative the investment is. However, the cap rate should not be the only factor in your decision-making. It should always be a piece of the puzzle, but do enough research to ensure that the investment is right for you. Cap rates vary drastically based on many factors, like location and the condition of the property. A cap rate of 9–10 percent is usually a fair compromise for both buyers and sellers. At this number, sellers can secure a reasonable market value for their properties, and buyers have a solid projected upside for their investment. But don't expect every party to be willing to sell at a 10 percent cap rate. A 10 percent cap rate typically won't provide a turnkey property either; those are usually properties that need some work, and the owners are no longer interested in making the changes themselves.

The Spread

Another important calculation you should know about is termed "the spread." The spread is a commonly used financial term that represents the difference between two prices, rates, or yields.

Let's look at the spread between cap rate and interest rate. This can be a good indicator of your future returns on the park. Here's an example to drive this home.

Let's say you're buying a park with an NOI of $100,000 per year and a market value of $1 million. That equates to a cap rate of 10 percent ($100,000 ÷ $1,000,000 × 100 = 10%), which isn't a bad investment. But before we go on, drill this into your mind: NOI encompasses all operating expenses but leaves out debt service, fees, and interest. This is critical to remember, as loan interest payments—a huge expense—aren't included when you calculate NOI or cap rate.

This is where the spread comes in. Let's say your interest rate on the loan is 7 percent. With the 10 percent cap rate, your spread on the property is the difference between your cap rate on the interest rate on the loan—in this case, only 3 percent. Does that change your mind on whether the RV park is a great deal? It should. You can see why the spread is such a critical number. What once looked like a great investment opportunity now appears to be a meager return on investment at best.

Increasing the Spread

I don't stop my analysis there, and you shouldn't either. The end goal is to try to maximize your spread on every property. In the previous example, I'd review the multitude of things I could do to increase the spread. Here are just a few:

- **Find cheaper money.** Banks will compete for your business, and I never assume I'm getting the best interest rate on a loan until I check out the competition.
- **Have a list of ways you can increase the NOI.** We talk about some of my favorite options to increase NOI once taking over a property later in this book.
- **Make a counteroffer.** If you assume the same cap rate and interest rate as above but you can get the property for $500,000, your cap rate soars to 20 percent, leaving you with a spread of 13 percent. That's a whole lot more attractive!

The spread is a very important number, and many deals will not make sense right away. You should look at what you can do to increase the spread and provide yourself with the greatest take-home profit possible.

Cash-on-Cash Return

Yet another important piece of the puzzle is the cash-on-cash return (CoC). This is what percentage of your down payment you're projected to return each year.

To best illustrate a CoC, let's go back to the example from above. You are considering a park at a price of $1 million, and let's say your local lender requires you to put down 30 percent cash. In other words, you had to come to the table with $300,000 in cash. Remember that the NOI is $100,000.

Your first thought may be *Holy smokes! That's a 33 percent CoC because the NOI is $100,000!* But this is a common miscalculation. A CoC return is calculated as your free cash flow *after* debt services, divided by initial cash outlay (or down payment). Mathematically, your equation would be:

CoC = (NOI – (Annual Cash Flow, Before Taxes)) ÷ Total Cash Investment in Property

Since your NOI never includes loan payments or any other debt-related fees, you need to calculate what you will pay for the loan, interest, and any other fees before you can calculate CoC.

Continuing with this example, we know our initial cash outlay is $300,000. We also know that our NOI is $100,000, but we must subtract our loan principal and interest payments. If we use the same 7 percent interest rate from the previous example on the $700,000 loan, we see that our annualized debt service cost is about $56,000. So, we subtract that $56,000 from our $100,000 NOI, which leaves us with an annual free cash flow of $44,000. When you divide the $44,000 by the $300,000 initial investment, you end up with, approximately, a 15 percent CoC. At that rate, it will take about six years to recoup your initial investment in the property.

Here is how this might look in a spreadsheet:

Value of Park	$1,000,000
Initial Investment (Down Payment)	$300,000
NOI	$100,000
Debt Service (Annual)	$56,000
Free Cash Flow (NOI – Debt Service)	$44,000
Cash-on-Cash Return (Free Cash Flow ÷ Initial Investment)	14.7%

A 15 percent CoC isn't bad, but I'd consider operational changes I could make to the property to increase that NOI, which would likewise increase the CoC. I would also look around for a better interest rate, and I may consider increasing the number of sites on the property. All of these would sweeten the deal.

I've seen RV park investor goals range from 8 to 20 percent CoC return; and of course, the higher the number, the better the deal. In the case of a 20 percent CoC, that means you will have earned your original deposit back in five years (assuming you put 20 percent down). I don't know too many people who would turn that down.

On the other hand, an 8 percent CoC return isn't enough for some investors, and 20 percent is very difficult to find. I typically shoot for about a 15 percent CoC. When you compare this to an average ten-year stock market return (currently around 10 percent),[4] 15 percent sounds like an amazing investment. This showcases how lucrative RV park investing can be for those who work hard and are willing to learn. While purchasing an RV park may take up a lot of your time and energy, if you look for opportunities that provide higher CoC, the investment can be unparalleled.

Number of Sites

The number of sites a park has directly correlates to its revenue potential and cash flow. Simply put, the more sites a park has, the more the park is worth. You can think of it like a parking garage. If you have 500 spots, you have the potential to make far more money than an equally positioned garage that has fifty spots.

With this in mind, nearly every park owner does their best to maximize the number of sites on their property. That number is often limited by physical constraints. You need room for the guests you are trying to attract to get in and out of the sites, and each site will vary in length and space needed for entry and exit (depending on the size of the RV).

When I look at expanding a park, I use the estimate of ten sites per acre as a maximum density rule of thumb. But that estimate greatly depends on topography, wetlands, or local zoning requirements due to setbacks. For example, a municipality might require that your RV park sign be placed at least twenty feet from the road. This setback would change the layout of the park and may change how much of the property is capable of being developed. This is why it is imperative to confirm your back-of-the-napkin estimates with hard numbers when you actually get into due diligence.

---

4   James Royal and Arielle O'Shea, "What Is the Average Stock Market Return?" Nerdwallet, March 5, 2024, https://www.nerdwallet.com/article/investing/average-stock-market-return.

For example, I went under contract to buy a property next to a park that I owned, and while going through due diligence, I learned that those adjacent ten acres had steep hills and a topography that would not permit development into RV sites without extensive costs for moving and filling with dirt. The cost of moving dirt alone was going to be $1 million. My due diligence allowed me to realize those adjacent acres would not make a good investment.

Due diligence allows you that deeper dive into the math based on the unique features of the land, local ordinances, actual drawings from civil engineers, and quotes from contractors. Only when your anticipated return on investment can be realized in the amount of time you expect does a deal make sense.

Local and state regulations can also constrain how many sites your RV park can have. Make sure you check with your local (city or county) planning and zoning department to see if a certain distance is required between each site. Additionally, check the National Fire Protection Association (NFPA) regulation 1194 as this contains health and safety codes for RV park construction.[5] It may have additional requirements.

In most cases, I place my sites as close as they're legally allowed to be to maximize the revenue from my developed land. Of course, you need to balance proximity with the atmosphere you want for your park. If your park is in a wooded, natural area, you will likely want to leave some trees as a barrier between sites.

Location

RV park values are closely tied to their location. Proximity to popular tourist attractions or a major city allows park owners to command substantially higher reservation fees than rural parks generate. Higher rates mean higher gross revenue and NOI, assuming your operating costs didn't increase by the same amount (due to higher wages, utilities, taxes, etc.). A higher NOI means a higher market value.

---

5 "NFPA 1194," National Fire Protection Association (NFPA), https://www.nfpa. org/codes-and-standards/all-codes-and-standards/list-of-codes-and-standards/ detail?code=1194.

Taking camping to the next level.

Upkeep

The RV park's condition also influences its market value. Owners defer maintenance expenses for any number of reasons, and this can be a blessing and a curse. Deferred maintenance is an accumulation of chores and upgrades to the property that previous owners have put off. These include things like fixing bathhouses, paving roads, improving amenities, or upgrading utilities. Deferring maintenance can lead to bigger, more expensive problems down the road, but this also gives you more leverage to strike a better deal for the property. Most property owners realize that these large expenses are coming up, which could make them more motivated to sell.

I approach these properties with the mindset that this a property to flip. You can point to these things and say, "If I buy this park, I need to make all of these investments to get it in decent shape, so I want this much deducted from the sales price." I'm typically quite excited to see parks with deferred maintenance. They are often in distress, and properties in distress present huge opportunities for buyers. However, it is important to obtain accurate estimates of the costs needed to bring the property back to its peak state. You must toe the line between getting a great deal on the purchase price and preventing yourself from buying a money pit.

Amenities

Park amenities often serve as substantial streams of income, and high-quality amenities allow owners to charge higher rates to their guests.

Reviewing specific P&L statements on an amenity-by-amenity basis allows you to understand what microbusinesses or revenue streams you're getting when you purchase a property. For example, if someone were to purchase one of my parks, they would be interested to know how much my golf cart rental business or the camp store is making each year. You can also use Chapter 11, which goes over amenities, to consider ideas to expand the current offerings.

Identifying Additional Opportunities

The value of your park can vary greatly depending on some additional factors that are identified below. It is important to consider each of these when you are reviewing a potential property and whether it has the potential to be more valuable with time.

Expansion Potential

If expanding your park is an option, be aware of how much time and effort it would cost to develop the land. It is critical that you add this to your due diligence. How long would it take to recoup that investment? These are important factors that will greatly impact what you offer for the property. Sellers can inflate the price of a park because of its alleged expansion potential, and you need to know if those prices are reasonable. Don't fall for this trap without confirming the numbers for yourself. As I shared earlier, I determined that one of my parks was *technically* expandable—it just required $1 million in dirt. That prohibitive cost meant that it wasn't truly expandable, and I had to assume the number of sites would not change.

Be bold and ask questions of the sellers regarding the land's value and potential. My first question in this regard is "Why haven't you developed additional sites yet?" Pay attention to the answer. If they are well capitalized and haven't made improvements, it is likely due to the enormous cost associated with the development.

Also, sellers won't always know the answer, and this usually has nothing to do with deceit. The seller may be an excellent park operator, but park development may not be their area of expertise. Or maybe they are simply content with what they have.

Operational Change Potential

If a park has a spectacular manager, great processes, fabulous reviews, and advanced technological amenities, you will likely pay a premium for the park, and there will be less room for growth. However, if the park doesn't have a good online presence, hasn't been using up-to-date marketing concepts, and is still taking reservations with pen and paper, the NOI is going to be lower, and you'll get it at a lower price. This is good news for you, as this represents a ton of upside that doesn't require a lot of up-front costs.

Poorly run parks give you an opportunity to increase efficiency, reduce costs, and ultimately drive up the NOI. While the park's existing cap rate may not be high, you can calculate a fair estimate of the future cap once you know the upside potential.

Evaluating Property Operations

Information on the competence of on-site management and the efficiency of organizational processes such as cleaning schedules and payment systems is nearly impossible to obtain without speaking with park employees. This information isn't always public or easy to obtain, but if you know what to look for, you will be able to make smarter, more informed investment decisions.

Be up front with sellers about the information you would like to access in order to make a competitive offer. The vast majority (I'd estimate 90 percent) of owners will refuse to give you access to their staff or customers. They typically don't want the risk of their staff quitting or their customers leaving once the gossip of management change starts. (And I assure you, it will start.) The owners will be concerned that if they show you around and you decide not to buy their property, it will significantly impact their business—and they are 100 percent right. So be respectful of them if they don't want to let out any inkling of a potential purchase.

Existing operations can also have varying value, depending on the buyer's intentions. Some buyers look for a park with a great team in place that they will simply take over, while others look to bring in or build their own teams.

Since I know that I can make operational improvements that will either save or make me more money, I consider a seller's inefficiencies my opportunity. To maximize your investment, examine all areas of operations to look for areas where you could immediately increase the value of the property. Some of these common low-hanging fruits are industry-specific operating software, great websites and social media presence, Google AdWords and pay-per-clicks, online reservation options, and many others that don't include heavy capital investments. Running an RV park is a business, so taking note of inefficiencies and then rapidly creating improvements will create quick, massive gains that increase the park's value.

I encourage you to look for these inefficiencies and consider in advance how you might capitalize on them. As an example, the first property I bought had been run as a long-term park when it was in a perfect location to be a short-term park. By converting it to a short-term park, I took it from a $3.2 million valuation to the $13 million value it has today.

Utilities

As you evaluate the value and operations of the park, consider who is paying for the utilities. Different parks do different things, and your evaluation could be entirely wrong if you assume customers pay for the utilities and later discover that the park is footing the bill.

RV parks generally provide water, sewer, and electricity to all their guests through hookups provided at each site. It's common to see short-term parks cover the costs of these expenses in their operations. However, long-term parks often require their tenants pay for utilities. Nevertheless, you want to be sure you know the arrangement before running your numbers.

Another important thing to determine is whether the park is on city water and sewer, or whether the park has private utilities. There are countless investors (including me) who won't buy a property if it's not on city water and sewer. Relying on private utilities can be extremely expensive. If disaster strikes, you'll likely be in for an enormous bill that will crush your entire operating income for the year. If you do find yourself pursuing a park that has private utilities, make sure you build in a huge margin, because your budget could very well require it.

If you are considering buying a park that has private utilities, you should absolutely have professional inspections done to make sure they are in good working order. In my opinion, even a 10 percent cap rate and a 20 percent CoC would not be nearly enough for me to take the chance on a property that's not on city water and sewer. Sometimes a septic system can be okay, but you must have it inspected first. I might make an exception if I learned that city utilities were available, but the owners hadn't been willing to pay the price to connect. In this case, I would run the numbers to see if the deal would still work out financially if I were to pay the connection fee.

Crunching Numbers

As useful as cap rates and related metrics can be, without some common sense, they can be incredibly misleading. Before you purchase, you'll want to determine whether or not additional investment is needed right away. This will include the prior owner's deferred maintenance that now affects the functioning of your park, or other immediate costs like software upgrades, marketing expenses, and new employee wages. Sometimes, properties need to have tens of thousands of dollars of work done to ensure continued operations, which affects the NOI for years.

Another pitfall for inexperienced RV park investors is not creating a realistic budget for the property they are considering. If you underestimate even just a few recurring costs, your cap rate and CoC will be skewed. This can quickly lead you into risky territory where you buy a property that costs more money than it makes.

The main takeaway from this section should be that cap rates, spreads, and CoC are useful ways to understand an RV park investment's potential. But if the operating costs and market value aren't calculated correctly, then you can be working with incorrect data, which can lead investors to make poor decisions. The next section peers into the critical analysis of operating costs.

Land Lease

Sometimes the current owner of an RV park doesn't actually own the land, but they have a lease and permission to operate the business there. This could still be a great business model if, for example, the land lease has ninety-nine years left. The value probably won't be impacted for decades.

But if only twenty or thirty years remain on the lease, the park's valuation will be very different. Moreover, appreciation works differently for leased land. With each loan payment, you are paying toward a lease rather than owning land that appreciates. For this reason, I don't buy properties that sit on leased land. Some investors do this, but it's not something I recommend.

Chapter 7

BUY OR BUILD
(THERE'S NO ONE WAY TO DO IT)

One of the questions I commonly get is whether it's better just to build a park instead of buying one. With a large enough parcel of land that is properly zoned, you may find yourself in a position where development could be incredibly lucrative. But before we go down this path, let me remind you of a huge factor: municipal utilities. As I stated previously, city water and sewage are critical to your valuation, so you need to understand your options before you even consider building. I'd even put it before permitting—it's that important.

If you can't hook up to city water and sewage, my advice is to walk away. For an inexperienced investor, taking the financial risk to install a private treatment facility is not advisable. You will run into challenges and probably bigger bills than you were quoted.

With that note of caution, let's assume you found a chunk of land that is hooked up to city utilities or can be for a price that fits in your numbers. You could be in for an awesome opportunity. Of course, you should refer back to all the information in the previous sections about cap rates, spreads, and CoC to model some scenarios in which your development is complete. But there is more to this than just forecasting future scenarios. You must understand the short-term impact on your investment.

One way to do this is to analyze the price per site of nearby parks to gauge your local development cost. If you can consider what other "comparable" parks are charging, and how your upgraded park might compare to their rates, you can gauge how long it will take to recoup any investments you are going to make in your own property. I believe this is a critical consideration when I review whether I can invest in a property and recoup my investment.

The easiest way to go through this is with an example. Let's say you're looking at a piece of land that is five minutes down the road from a short-term RV park, and you want to build a competing park. The park down the road has 200 sites and a market value of $2 million. This means that the market value per site at the neighboring park is $10,000. Of course, these are hypothetical numbers, but we are using them as an example at this point.

Turning to your own property, when you go through your due diligence process for the development of your competing park, you must determine if you can get the price per site of your park at or below $10,000. If you're planning to build an entirely different type of property from your competitor, and your amenities and expenses can command higher rates, this metric isn't as helpful because you would ultimately be generating more revenue per site. But assuming the parks will be similar, $10,000 per site is a good litmus test.

Here's how you can estimate costs for a park that hasn't been built. First, look at the price of land, and second, look at the price of development. Getting the price of the land is the easiest step. You call the broker and ask what they want for the parcel you are considering and negotiate accordingly.

The second factor is where it gets tricky. What will you spend to develop the park? One significant cost is excavation work. You'll need sewer lines, water, electricity, paving, and construction of your supporting facilities. Then you'll need Wi-Fi and the various other amenities that will set you apart. For all of this, the best place to start is with professional civil engineer drawings. You will need to engage a civil engineer—and an industry-specific, local engineer will typically be the best choice. If you couldn't find both industry-specific *and* local, I would err on the side of industry-specific. That may result in you needing to hire a local zoning expert to assist the civil engineer.

If you're thinking about taking on a large project, I'd recommend working with a seasoned industry expert who can help you through the planning stages, so you can accurately price each and every aspect of development. For the best estimate, you should get contractor quotes on everything. I always add in a buffer of 10 percent just in case costs run over.

Let's turn back to our example. Let's say the parcel of land you're targeting has an asking price of $500,000. Then, let's assume that you will pay $400,000 to get all your utilities set up, $300,000 for excavation, and $500,000 in construction costs for 200 sites. The total cost of the project is $1.7 million.

Let's assume that it will take two years to complete the project, so you will have two years of debt payments without the park generating revenue. If you can come to the table with $500,000 in cash to start the project, you will need a loan of $1.2 million. Using a 5 percent interest rate as an example, which may or may not be applicable when you read this book, a 5 percent interest rate will add an additional $100,000 or so, bringing your total project cost to a little over $1.8 million. The neighboring park was valued at $2 million with 200 sites for the price per site of $10,000. In this example, developing your park would result in a price per site of about $9,000. Because the price per site is lower for a newly built park, it could make a lot of sense. Keep in mind that this is an example based on a park similar to the competing park down the road. If you're trying to build a park that provides a unique customer experience in the area, you should be willing to pay more per site because you plan to extract more value per site.

Also, remember that this two-year investment of time and resources has an opportunity cost; you could have been making money had you bought a park that was already operational. All things being equal between a nearby park and a development project, it likely makes more sense to buy an existing park rather than trying to develop your own. You will see better returns immediately, and you won't have to worry about the headache and time required to develop the land.

Site Types

There are many site types to consider as you develop your RV park. We'll go into the specifics in a future chapter, but it is important to consider the site types as you begin thinking about developing the park from the dirt up. A typical RV park will have single sites, which are positioned so that everyone is parked in the same direction. This creates an extra privacy screen from the neighboring campers.

Buddy sites are currently a popular trend and allow for different opportunities for your site setup. One site is positioned in the normal direction and a second site is positioned backward. In this scenario, the camper doors face each other. One camper will park backward in the buddy site. This means that the utilities for that camper will need to be on the reverse side. This configuration is desirable for some because it allows people who are camping in a group to socialize together under their awnings instead of facing opposite directions. For this reason, if you're developing a new park or expanding an old one, you may want to consider building a few buddy sites.

Pull-through sites are another great option to consider when developing your park. These sites have a road on both ends, which means your guests never have to back in to their site. Whether it's fueled by all the new campers who hate backing in or just the ease of use, we're definitely seeing higher demand for pull-through sites.

There are also opportunities for nontraditional site development, which include permanent structures (like glamping tents, yurts, tree houses, domes, tiny homes, and remodeled train cars).

RV Park—Specific Tools

If you plan to develop or expand a park, make sure that you have a copy of the NFPA 1194. This construction code provides all kinds of useful information for developing an RV park property. It's also important to use civil engineers and consultants who are familiar with the RV park and campground industries specifically, not just somebody who has done hotel or other commercial development. Those with industry-specific experience will know things that you won't catch, for example, what Good Sam requires for good ratings, or what layout best facilitates camper experience. I've purchased a property from someone who did not use industry-specific engineers or consultants, and I ended up having to dig up the sites at a cost of $10,000 per site just so I could redesign and repave the grounds to meet code. You will save a huge headache and a ton of money by using industry-specific consultants.

Zoning

Zoning relates to the rules that may exist as to how you can use your property. Zoning laws vary across the country, so you also want any engineers, contractors, or consultants to have experience in the locale of your park because they'll be able to work with city planning and zoning instead of you. I can tell you from experience that zoning can be very frustrating.

Each city has its own ordinances and requirements for zoning and permitting for different asset classes and different commercial buildings. Each detail of what you do is determined by what the city requires, and details can be as restrictive as how far from the road a sign must be posted, whether you can use gravel in your campground, or if you must pave it with rebar. (These are all true stories from my campgrounds.) If you buy a property without knowing the local rules and zoning restrictions, or the prior owner did something that wasn't permitted, you may have to tear out all of those improvements and start over.

Expansion

When you're considering a property, whether it's land for development or a campground that has room for expansion, make sure you know how much of that land is usable. You may have a beautiful area of the park that seems ideal for development, but the government has designated it a wetland. That means it's great to look at, but you can't use to it make any money.

Your next consideration should be the cost. Using the example from earlier, where the topography of the land required $1 million in dirt alone to level the area enough to put RV sites on it, you could easily be pushed out of your budgeted price range. And again, that didn't include adding extra amenities to accommodate for more sites.

In short, no matter what property you are considering, do your research. Do your due diligence. If you don't do it up front, you are rolling the dice with your investment—and I don't want to see you gamble it away.

Letter of Intent

Once you have fully evaluated a property and are confident in your numbers, it's time to write a letter of intent, or LOI, to the current property owner. This document is nonbinding (so both parties can walk away), and it doesn't need to be complex. All your letter of intent does is set forth a basic, initial agreement between you and the seller. If the seller needs to seek legal counsel to help them understand your LOI, you've gone too far. Binding legal arrangements will be handled in your purchase and sale agreement, or PSA. Your LOI should avoid big words and technical jargon that will confuse the seller. Make the terms as clear as possible regarding earnest money, price, closing date, the due diligence period, and how you plan to pay for the transaction. The rest of the details can be left for the PSA.

Keep in mind that if you're actively pursuing an RV park investment, you'll be writing quite a few letters of intent. Spending too much time on legal jargon and technical language will slow you down and hold you back from evaluating deals and sending out offers.

Chapter 8

FINANCING RV PARKS

inancing is no one's idea of a picnic. Many people get nervous about it, and for many, it's the most complicated, anxiety-inducing step of the entire purchasing process. But it doesn't have to be.

My goal in this chapter is to share with you all the variations the financing step might entail and to give you an idea of the curveballs you may encounter. After all, if you know almost everything that could come your way, you have little to worry about and a minimal chance of surprises.

Remember this first and foremost: Every financing deal is unique. This is not a cookie-cutter process. I could close on ten properties in a row, and every financing package would be different in some way—a different structure, a different property, a different buyer with different needs, and sometimes even a different investor.

Let's start by reviewing the various methods of financing and how each can apply to the wildly varying scenarios out there. By the end of this chapter, you will understand the pros and cons of each type of financing, from traditional lending (using local banks and credit unions) to private money and partners. I'll also share game plans you can use to discover which type of financing is best for your scenario and the smartest practices you can adopt during the financing step. I'm also showing you the latest techniques employed by the most experienced RV park investors and the common traps to avoid.

Commercial Lending via Local Banks

Most seasoned real estate investors will tell you that one of the most important first steps is securing financing. I suggest using local banks and credit unions for this step. In contrast to loans through institutional residential lenders (a process you're probably familiar with), commercial lending typically involves local banks or credit unions. Because these companies are local, you can realize several benefits.

Benefits of Local Banks

First, they offer flexibility. These smaller institutions thrive on relationships, and their leadership structure is usually small enough to allow the decision-makers to know the borrower. So, you will probably meet the loan officer and even the bank's manager—two people from your community who have decision-making authority and can guide you on what they are seeking and what rules they can bend. That's an opportunity you will rarely get at a bank with a national scope.

Local banks and credit unions also know that long-term, local customers are their bread and butter. As they get to know you, they will be even more inclined to be flexible. Perhaps they know that you have kept a perfect record with them in the past, and they believe you are a safe bet. Or maybe their kid plays baseball with your kid, and they respect your positive approach to parenting. Whatever the reason, local banks make decisions locally, meaning your relationship with them can change everything.

For example, it's not uncommon for park owners to refuse to show their books unless you have a preapproval letter in hand from a bank. But with large banks, getting that letter will require information, documentation, and probably a lot of time. I've been able to get a preapproval letter from my local banks with merely a text message to one of the bankers I work with regularly. Of course, the standard process for approval will still apply in the next stage of the purchase, but this speedy preapproval letter can make all the difference in a hot market. If it's a great property, you could be competing with other buyers for the deal, and every day counts.

A second benefit to local banks is they will often have packages that national banks would never offer. I've found this to be true with RV parks in particular. Many of the institutional giants refuse to grant loans on RV parks, but local banks will find a way.

As an example, a few years back, I attended a conference at which Wells Fargo was marketing to people investing in mobile home parks.

Surprised to hear that this national bank was lending to mobile home park investors, I asked if they had options for RV park investors. They did not. Unfortunately, I've found this to be quite common among the largest national banks.

Three Detriments of Park Financing

I told you I'd share everything I know, so I'll likewise divulge the potential drawbacks to using these smaller, local banks and credit unions.

The first drawback is that smaller banks may not be willing to work outside of a certain geographical area that they serve. They are locally focused, and as a result, they sometimes draw boundaries within the areas that they know and serve. Local banks have the distinct advantage of knowing their service area better than national banks; and they tend to keep their focus on that area they know best.

Second, as a borrower, you can end up with higher interest rates. Local banks generally have a strict approval process and nearly always lack the resiliency of larger banks because their investments are not spread widely across many economic zones. In other words, if something upsets the applecart in the primary service area of Anytown, USA, the bank could go under. For this reason, your loan with Anytown Bank can be riskier than the same loan with Bank of America. Anytown Bank adjusts the interest rate accordingly to accommodate their increased risk.

Third, traditional lenders may not be familiar with RV park and campground investments, which means they might be unwilling to finance the venture. If this happens, look for community banks that have other RV parks and campgrounds in their service area.

Summary

Despite these three possible drawbacks, I encourage you to put traditional lending options toward the top of your list. Start where your prospective property is located and search for the banks and credit unions in that county, then call each of them to speak with a loan officer. I find this personalized approach to be a game changer.

I also encourage you not to give up, even if the first few banks don't offer what you're seeking. Be persistent, just as you have been with your efforts in locating properties. The persistent investors find the opportunities. Once you find a good bank, you'll learn that one of the greatest advantages of using a local option is the bank's familiarity with the area.

Hopefully, the lender will also know something about the asset class. My entire portfolio is currently financed either directly through the owner or with a local bank.

Remember that buying an RV park requires a commercial loan and will likely involve a 20–30 percent down payment. But rather than a home or residency, you're purchasing a business. Banks expect a greater percentage of investment in commercial properties, and if you keep your commitments, your relationships will prosper.

Private Money

Another alternative for purchasing an RV park or campground is funding your deal with private money. Before we get too far in the weeds on this, I want to be clear that there are two types of private money: equity and debt.

Here's a quick example of why you might finance an entire deal with private money. Let's say you're trying to buy a campground for $10 million, and the bank you're working with wants you to come to the table with $3 million. If you don't have $3 million cash to put into the deal, you'll need to raise private money to come up with whatever chunk of the $3 million you can't bring on your own. Private money investors can supply you with the cash you need to bring to the table—for a price.

There are no set rules in private money lending. Sometimes private money is used as debt, and sometimes it is used as equity. Regardless of which side of the deal you land on in this regard, you will need proper legal representation and documentation to make sure you understand the ramifications of the private money agreement you are considering.

To sum this up, you could buy a $10 million campground with $3 million of private money and $7 million of traditional (bank) lending. If the agreement for the $3 million of private money is in debt, you will have terms that are similar to a bank: Once you pay them back, the property is yours, free and clear. If, instead, the $3 million is in equity, the lender will likely own a percentage of the property.

Working with private money comes with a whole new set of challenges that are beyond the scope of what I cover in this book, but you should know that private investors often try to sweeten the deal for themselves and lower the risk on their investment as much as possible. Because these types of deals can fall underneath the Securities and Exchange Commission (SEC), you need to be sure to engage an attorney with SEC knowledge to review your private money agreements. Whenever you use private money, be sure you appropriately factor in all the private money terms into the underwriting for your deal.

You're probably wondering: When does private money make sense? On the equity side, it makes sense when you have a great deal that you can't afford to buy on your own. On the debt side, it makes sense for simple remodels or expansion projects that banks are less likely to lend on, especially if the project is quick and you can tolerate the high interest rate. But generally speaking, you're better off taking on debt from conventional sources, as interest rates will almost always be cheaper at a bank than with private lenders. The catch here is that the bank might not be willing to lend for every deal, which may force you down the private debt route. If this happens, double-check that your deal still works with more expensive debt service payments.

Always Remember the Spread

Recall that the spread is the difference between your cap rate (or ROI) and your interest rate. Calculate the spread with every offer you have to make sure you aren't losing money or barely scraping by each month. It helps to have three years of P&L statements to validate the previous owner's claims.

Finally, make sure your deal has some of the huge upsides we've discussed (like room for expansion or upgraded amenities) because you will want to refinance eventually to get out of the private lender's high interest rate. If you must start out with a high interest rate, make sure you have a plan to change it in the future. But even situations like this can be beneficial in the long run.

Partners

Yet another way to invest in an RV park or campground is through a partnership. Let's say, for example, that you were unable to qualify for a conventional loan, and you don't have access to private money. Your interest in RV parks doesn't need to be put on hold! A partnership could be a great way for you to get started in the space.

The best partnerships have two or more partners who each bring something unique to the table. A common way to structure a partnership is where one party brings the money to fund the deal while the other party does the work of finding, purchasing, and managing the property. However, partnerships can be structured and negotiated in countless ways.

After reading this book, you will know how to find deals, evaluate them, and properly operate them once you close. You now have a valuable skill set that almost no one has—you just need to leverage it. Here's how.

Go out and do the work to find the RV park deals. Call owners and request the offering memorandums (OMs) and any other data you need to evaluate the opportunity.

Once you get there, take the information to your network. (I'd encourage networking through the entire process too.) Start with the friends and family you know well, then consider branching out to people outside of your close network. Networking to find partners is a skill set in itself. There are multiple sources you can turn to in this regard, including *Raising Private Capital* by Matt Faircloth.[6] If you have done your homework properly and the numbers are truly attractive, someone will be willing to partner with you.

When you structure your new partnership, make sure that every detail is accounted for. Who is responsible for running the park? If a major expense comes up and the park can't fund it, who pays? Who determines when to make capital improvements? All these small details will impact the success of the park and your partnership. Be sure to have all these items clearly spelled out in your operating agreement before signing anything. It's best practice to have your own legal counsel review your operating agreement so that your interests are appropriately represented and protected.

Owner Financing

Owner financing can be a good option for buyers who don't qualify for traditional loans. This financing method is similar to private money in that the mortgage is held with a private entity rather than a bank. However, with owner financing, the previous owner of the property holds the note. This means that the lender sets their own terms for the down payment, interest rate, repayment schedule, as well as the consequences of defaulting on the loan. In most owner-financed loans, a common arrangement is to amortize the loan over thirty years to keep the monthly payments low, with a final balloon payment due in three,

---

6   You can purchase Matt's book at www.biggerpockets.com/store.

five, or ten years. By that point, the new owner will have (hopefully) built enough equity on the property to refinance out of the remaining balance of the loan with a traditional lender. You'd be surprised how many campground owners will consider this option when you show how quickly you will be buying them out and how much money they will make in interest payments.

Small Business Administration (SBA)

The SBA can be a valuable agency for many small business owners. It has numerous free resources that include everything from business guides to funding programs to educational webinars for small business owners. I encourage you to explore their resources if you haven't already been exposed to them from previous ventures. The SBA tends to have low down payment options, such as 10 percent in many cases, and they have long repayment terms and protection from balloon payments. The loans can also include "soft costs," such as furniture, fixtures, and fees.

And while the SBA can be advantageous in some ways, keep in mind there can also be some detriments to working with the SBA. While I have never personally used an SBA loan, my mastermind students who have used these types of loans have talked about the intense amount of documentation required and the length of time it can take to close a loan. In some cases, it has taken more than a year to close. I would recommend you explore and consider other options if you run into roadblocks like long closing deadlines and lengthy documentation collection timelines.

Independence Bank

Independence Bank has been specializing in campground lending since 2002. In the event you want to consider buying a KOA investment, you may want to check out Independence Bank as a lender. KOA, or Kampgrounds of America, is a large network of privately owned campgrounds with nearly 500 locations across the United States and Canada. Independence Bank finances over 40 percent of active KOA campgrounds with more than $300 million in loans on the books to KOA franchise owners.

Independence Bank's vast experience with campground financing and lending provides a huge advantage for prospective buyers. They also offer competitive interest rates, amortizations, and nonrepayment penalties. They can create customizable payment schedules, and they have offerings in Small Business Administration (SBA) 504 financing. When it comes to developing and improving a property, Independence Bank also offers supplementary financing with a quick approval process, no cash down, flexible payment schedules, and repayments based on revenue or camper nights. I'm not one to limit my potential acquisition options to a single brand (KOA in this case), but Independence Bank brings so many advantages to the table that it's hard to ignore.

Chapter 9

BEFORE CLOSING ON YOUR RV PARK

C ongratulations! You're about to become the owner of your very own RV park! After spending countless hours narrowing down properties and evaluating each option, you deserve some celebration. But the work isn't done yet. Despite the name, closing day is merely the beginning of your new adventure.

First, you'll need to prepare for a smooth transfer of ownership for the property. By following the suggestions in this chapter, you will do everything needed to ensure that business continues as usual at your park.

There is quite a bit to prepare for, so keeping a checklist will help you confirm when each process is complete. Some necessary checklist items include the following:

- Vendor contacts
- Social media account information
- Website log-ins
- Domain transfers
- Customer data
- Software data and log-ins
- Employee contacts
- Park keys
- Utility billing
- Shutoff locations in the park

- Existing leases
- The previous owner's contact information

I also suggest sending this list to the seller well in advance of signing day, so they can weigh in on whether you are missing any critical materials. The seller will know every important piece of information about the property and (given their similar desire to ensure the sale goes off without a hitch) has a vested interest in making sure your list is complete. Since missing just one critical item will cause delays and lost revenue, I encourage setting up a phone call to go over the list together. Use that opportunity to ask questions, go down the list one item at a time, get the seller's forwarding address and future contact info, and perhaps schedule a follow-up chat in a month or two just in case unforeseen questions arise.

Now, let's do a deeper dive on some of the items on your list.

Things to Get from the Seller

The following are the items that I make sure to bring up with the seller before I head into the closing. Gathering this information now will save you many headaches later, so you should not feel shy about asking for them.

Vendors

Campgrounds need vendors such as contractors, food suppliers, and linen suppliers. Each of these providers helps keep your park running. So instead of recreating the list yourself, ask your seller about the vendors they use and whether there are any issues or delivery schedules you should be aware of. I also encourage reaching out to the vendors directly well in advance of the transition, so services can continue uninterrupted and without any surprises.

More seasoned investors may already have a list of established vendors. However, I still value learning who the current owners use, so I can compare each vendor's pricing and negotiate deals to fit my needs and budget.

Note that some vendors may appear on the list only because they've been filling the role for years, not because they are the best choice. In addition to price, consider whether the vendor offers the best technology or product for your investment. For example, some campgrounds have antiquated wireless networks or inadequate security. So while those vendors might be cheap, they probably aren't the best ones for the job. Inspect the previous owner's vendor list, but get second opinions by bringing in potential suitors to bid as well.

Digital Assets

Digital assets encompass things like domain names, websites, and social media accounts—anything that is stored digitally and provides value (such as advertising) to the park. If you're not sure what digital assets the park has, start by asking questions: How does the park get business? What social media accounts platforms does it use? How does it currently advertise?

If social media makes you want to dive off a cliff, let me talk you off the ledge. First and foremost, you will likely not be starting from scratch. Most RV parks and campgrounds have built some kind of online following, and it usually makes sense to build on what already exists. To ensure the easiest transfer, add account access and passwords to the list of items you need from the previous owners. You will also want to alter the security questions and emergency contacts for these accounts once you have taken the reins.

Also, make sure to get administrative passwords for the park's advertising accounts, website(s), internal software, and other digital products. Confirm that your access works and that it has administrator access, which is often required to make any significant changes. You can modify things later by adding your own flair, style, and preferences.

In the case of web hosting, you should expect to transfer the hosting to your account rather than take over their account. This grants you full control and a clean transfer. There are literally hundreds of options for web hosts, such as GoDaddy or Cloudflare, but the last thing you want is to have the website become inaccessible because of poor planning. If you've never hosted a website before, I'd encourage paying the small extra fee to have your future host transfer it over. It's far more expensive and difficult to rebuild a site than to transfer an old one, so take the easy route. You can revisit your website in the months after closing.

Some previous owners may be reluctant to go through this technical process because it can be time consuming. Yet it is essential for your domain account transfer to be a success. Otherwise, you will need to build your website and online presence from scratch, which could take years and confuse previous customers who likely won't understand the name change. Completing this transfer will also allow many new guests to easily find you when they perform a Google search, which will help your park grow.

Data

For a smooth transfer, you'll need to gather the park's employee and customer data. Both play roles in helping you succeed as an RV park owner. Employee data is necessary if you are moving to a new payroll system, but it's also good information to have for connecting you to your new staff before getting things started. As with most businesses, getting to know your employees will help you organize work and form beneficial relationships with them.

While employee data is important, customer data is even more important. Make sure you receive all customer information that the previous owners collected, such as email addresses and phone numbers, so you can start marketing to those who have already been to the property. This data can be extremely useful to drive your first sales campaign. For example, you may want to start with an email to previous guests announcing the park's new ownership and goals for improvements. This is a great way to grab your first few bookings at your new park.

As an added benefit, existing customer data can establish a baseline of customers from which the savvy marketer on your team can expand your audience. With a good dataset, you can target ads to people with interests and characteristics that are similar to those of previous customers.

You will also want access to the park's software system, even if you don't plan to use the same one. With this access, you can remove the previous ownership group from the system and install your own administrative controls. Request software system reports from prior years, so you have a baseline to reference during your first year of operations. Don't assume you've been given all the most relevant reports that you'll want to use for comparisons. By having access to the software, you can create whatever reports you need.

Keys, Utilities, Shutoff Locations, and Owner Contacts (Again)

The final items on the list are simple but easily forgotten. Don't forget the keys to everything on your property: buildings such as the amenities, storage facilities, bathhouses, and offices. Depending on the number of buildings and locks on your property, you may want to label all of them, so you don't have to rummage through a bunch of keys when you need one.

Also, change all the utilities to be under your name and contact information. That way, you're immediately responsible for paying the bills, and you won't risk the old owner being upset with you because they're still being charged for electrical service. Make a list of all the utilities the park uses, then check with the previous owner to make sure you haven't forgotten any. In the worst-case scenario, the old owner could (rightfully) opt not to pay a bill, risking a disconnection and service interruption to your guests.

While on the topic of utilities, ask where the shutoff valves are. You will eventually want to know, and it just saves time to ask the previous owner.

Finally, I will reiterate the importance of having correct contact info for the previous owners. If you ever have questions about the property, passwords, media information, or logistics, the easiest solution is to call the previous owner.

I know I've laid out a sizable checklist, but it's good to be prepared for every situation that may greet you. You can find a supplemental checklist at www.biggerpockets.com/campgroundbonus. If you've checked all these items off and talked with the seller about any other necessary processes, you should be good to go for closing day.

Once you can confirm that everything is in order, acknowledge your success. Book your favorite restaurant and treat yourself. You did it! You are officially the owner of an RV park.

Section II
UPGRADES AND ULTIMATE EXPERIENCES

Chapter 10

DETERMINING YOUR ACCOMMODATIONS

When it comes to alternative accommodations—any accommodation at an RV park that is not simply an RV site—you have a myriad of options. There are glamping tents, luxury glamping tents, rental campers, camping cabins, tiny homes, tree houses, yurts, and Hobbit homes (these are remodeled buses and train cars that have been turned into magical spaces). When choosing your alternative accommodations, pick something unique that you like and figure out how to make it an experience.

Cabins

Camping cabins are a popular alternative accommodation option. For most RV parks, cabins need to be RVIA (Recreational Vehicle Industry Association) certified. These are made by a certified manufacturer and have a seal of certification like you would find on a camper. The seal implies that the cabin has been inspected and certified by the agency. Cabins can then be approved by your planning and zoning commission.

Building your own cabin requires a different set of permits, and sometimes this is not allowed in an RV park because of building codes.

As they are RVIA certified, cabins are technically towable because they were manufactured at an RV facility and can be pulled down the road, just like a camper. These look like cabins to your customers, and they fit the vibe of the tiny home craze. Also, to receive RVIA certification, cabins must be under 399 sq. ft.

I added the cabins to one of my properties about eight years ago. I did this to bring in people who were looking for a unique camping experience but were not quite ready to purchase an RV. They were interested in camping while enjoying the amenities of a swimming pool and fishing ponds. Adding cabins will give you a different market to target. These cabins (I have about twenty of them) brought in about $500,000 over a twelve-month period, even though we were closed for a short time because of COVID.

Cabins are meant for short-term rentals, and they're comparable to an Airbnb-style rental. A lot of people who own vacation rentals use the Airbnb platform for payment. But because you're already spending the money marketing your property, coordinating reservations, and taking payments, you don't need Airbnb to rent these. Essentially, you can run a short-term rental program without Airbnb's service fees.

Cabin rentals are popular for people who are going on family vacations. They want to travel with different family members but do not want to room together. These cabins allow families to stay close but not in the same space. They also work for groups, such as rallies, baseball teams, and small parties, who travel together but don't have a camper. Cabins are also ideal for people who travel with their camper buddies but don't own a camper themselves.

A long time ago, camping cabins were bare bones, built mostly for KOAs. They had beds and maybe heating and air conditioning but no running water. But today's customer demands something a lot different. Modern camping cabins are similar to hotel accommodations, with heat, air conditioning, kitchens, bathrooms, and nice linens on those beds. Renters also expect things like shampoo, conditioner, soap, and dish soap. But with cabins, people are looking for that unique experience where they can still go camping, hiking, swimming, or have outdoor experiences they wouldn't have if they'd stayed in a hotel.

When picking out alternative accommodations, don't provide just one of something. Have multiples to accommodate groups of travelers. Even if you have multiple cabins, make sure they have the same layout. At one of my properties, sixteen of my twenty cabins have the same layout. As a result, when people make a reservation, they aren't reserving one specific cabin; they're reserving that cabin type, so I can shift who gets what cabin based on group sizes. This allows me to maximize occupancy, as well as my income.

Tents

As an alternate accommodation, tents are on the lower end of the spectrum. This is in contrast to "glamping," or glamorous camping, which I discuss in more detail below. Because tent campers spend most of their time outside, outdoor space is very important. With that in mind, we added a privacy fence around each tent. It doesn't look like much, but it's better than being close to the next tent. You might wonder, *Why don't you just give them more space?* Because this camping property is in a tourist town, land values are very high, and there is only so much space you can give up without charging too high a price. So adding the privacy fence was the best solution. Adding a firepit is a nice touch. Firepits allow customers to sit outside, use a grill, and have the option to cook.

At 100 percent occupancy, things can get a little crowded, because people bring a lot of things with them. Campers often bring their own outdoor camping chairs that they can use around the pool or fishing ponds. We anticipate this and provide a picnic table and chairs with each tent.

The financial return on this investment has been great. I had fifteen tents take in about $170,000 over twelve months. That figure would have been much higher if I hadn't waited until halfway through the season to raise our rates. With the development cost of around $225,000, it only took me a year and a half to realize a financial return on my initial investment.

There are two different sizes of glamping tents: two- and five-person tents. Smaller glamping tents have queen beds with hotel-quality mattresses and linens. They also have a single-serve coffee machine with a couple of coffee pods. Glamping tents have linens for cooking, for the restroom, for showering, and for use in the pools. They have electricity, as well as heat and air conditioning. These are closed for two months when the property is offseason. (When the temperatures reach down into the teens, the heaters just can't keep up.)

I also purchased ten tents that are meant for a family and can sleep five people. They have bunk beds in them, but they still have Appalachian log furniture, hotel-quality mattresses and linens, coffee machine, linens, soap, and shampoo for use in the bathhouse. They have full bathrooms, full kitchens, and provide the unique experience that your glamping customers are looking for. Depending on the area and time of year, these tents can bring in anywhere from $200 to $500 per night.

Rental RVs

Rental campers have been a huge craze over the last few years, and some very successful businesses have grown out of this demand, such as RVshare and Outdoorsy. These are website listing services for those who are not using their camper year-round and wish to rent it out. I own the campers that I rent out, as well as my websites. As a result, my numbers work out a little differently than somebody who simply rents out their camper with one of these services. My campers cost between $30,000 and $35,000 to purchase, and they bring in about $30,000 a year. That's a very quick return on your investment.

You'll want all your campers to have the same setup because, like we talked about with dynamic pricing and software, you'll want to maximize occupancy with your rates. Plan for each camper to sleep six people.

A rental camper is a great alternative accommodation because it has a low price point. Also, people who are considering buying a camper will want to stay in one for a couple nights before they make that big purchase.

Tiny Home

For glamping and alternative accommodations, camping cabins are tiny homes that cover a wide variety of options. With all the media attention around tiny homes, it has become a huge trend. So, when you're considering different types of accommodations for your glamping resort, these are a great option.

One of my first "tiny homes"—purchased before they were cool.

Alternative Accommodations and Pets

Most pet owners are extremely attached to their furry companions, so when it's time to go on vacation, plenty of people bring their pets. That means they will be looking for an RV park that accommodates their fur babies.

In my experience, most parks allow RVs with pets on board. I don't think I've been to one that didn't allow pets in campers. But for alternative accommodations, you will need to decide what you are comfortable with. If you allow pets, I recommend charging a pet fee, which can be as high as $50 a night. Note that not all accommodations are pet friendly. For example, some canvas tents are expensive to replace, and you don't want somebody's pet to scratch a hole in one. This would cause you to lose revenue while you complete the repairs, and your guests would be upset that they had to pay for the damage. It's also very hard to remove pet hair from canvas tents. For this reason, I don't accommodate pets in my glamping tents.

Also, check the laws that apply to emotional support animals and service animals, because the regulations are different for these two. The Americans with Disabilities Act governs the use and treatment of service animals, but not emotional support animals. Note that it is not legal to ask your guests certain questions about their service animals. Make sure you know the laws when setting your pet policies, and ask an industry-specific attorney when in doubt.

When camping with pets, the owner should sign a waiver. This is not just for the damage pets can do to your property; it's also in case a pet exhibits aggressive behavior and/or attacks another guest. By signing a waiver (prepared by an industry-specific attorney), you reduce your liability for the attack. No one likes to talk about a pet's potential to do harm, but you cannot predict what's going to happen.

I'm saying this from experience, as I have had multiple issues with pets. A couple years ago, I had a fabulous maintenance man who was asked to check the cabins after guests had checked out. When someone appears to be slow to check out, I usually ask my staff to nicely knock on their door and see if we can help them with anything. This is always done as a customer service.

When our maintenance man knocked, a German shepherd jumped through the screen door of the camper and bit his arm. The dog severed his artery, and blood was everywhere. I eventually paid a huge medical bill at the local hospital, mostly because the maintenance person was my employee, and I did not have a workers' comp policy. In short, have the proper legal documents signed before you let pets on the premises. These animals are not yours, and I have found that guests will tell you anything you want to hear to get permission to have a pet.

Note that in this case, the owner may have been technically responsible, but I chose not to sue the owner. Aside from it being bad policy—to sue guests for accidents—the cost of suing them will often be more than the bill itself. And that doesn't take into account the time and grief you will endure when you sue someone. Absent extreme cases, I avoid suing campers.

Glamping

This is a great amenity to consider, because glamping is growing tremendously in popularity. Glamping differs from camping in the type of accommodations, how furnished the tent is, what amenities are included in the tent, etc. And this heavily impacts the pricing.

For my properties, I use high-end, luxury safari tents from Tent Masters, but that is only one of many types. Glamping might also be done in yurts (portable, round tents supported by an angled assembly of latticework), Conestoga-style wagons, PlainsCraft covered wagons, teepees, and even tree houses. Although there are many ways to experience glamping, the focus is on experiencing nature in a more luxurious, unique fashion.

What is the real difference between camping and glamping? Let's say you are a huge hiking fan, on the trail whenever the weather permits. You can carry your tent and set it up along the way or find places that have glamping options. Glamping is all the outdoor fun of camping, but without all the hassle of pitching a tent or sleeping on the ground. Glamping also creates a more memorable experience than staying at a ho-hum hotel. If I fly into places, I likely won't remember a hotel stay twenty or thirty years down the road, but I will certainly remember a glamping experience. And in the hospitality industry, the experience is everything.

How posh are glamping options? Think jacuzzies, European rain showers, multiple bedrooms, multiple stories, sinks, mattresses, and, of course, toilets. Do the research and see what is out there, then create your own identity. There are many types of RV resorts and campgrounds, and some offer a glamping experience by starting off with maybe four or five units. They create their own style, whether it be in wagons, yurts, teepees, or safari tents.

Who is going glamping? This vacation trend has become quite a hit with younger generations. They tend to love nature, and they generally stay away from mainstream hotels. They love new and different experiences. For these people, nature and glamping go hand in hand.

I've met people who were completely moved by glamping. I know someone who most would call a city slicker. He was the kind of person who sees no purpose for camping. Six months into the pandemic, he went camping for the first time and loved it. He had been holed up for so long, he wanted to do something outside—something involving nature. He went out into the woods to see something new and beautiful. And it was transformative.

Consider installing high-end tents for glamping.

In the past few years, more and more people have wanted to return to nature—and that's not just true for Gen Zers and millennials. We've seen older folks who used to go camping returning to the woods. Maybe they aren't up for sleeping on the ground anymore, and that's when glamping comes into play. You provide them with a way to experience nature, but with a luxurious mattress, a shower, a gas stove, etc.

Weather conditions will affect what you can offer your glamping guests. Tents may not be appropriate in northern Canada or the rainforests of Costa Rica, but various forms of glamping thrive in those locations.

As with houses, there are different heating and cooling options available. No matter where you're located, there will be specialized accommodations that can help you deal with the environment. Let's say you have a glamping facility in Knoxville, Tennessee, as I do. It is possible to stay in one of the tents during the winter months, but at the end of the day, it's still a tent. Will it be as comfortable as a cabin, a house, or even an RV? Maybe not, but you can still keep it warm and toasty.

One option for keeping tents warm in winter is called radiant heating. This uses pipes that funnel hot water through a boiler, then through the floor. You need to pour concrete on top and cover it with tile or linoleum. Tile is usually preferred, and it enables you to use a wood, gas, or pellet stove. However, this solution is far more complex than just plugging in a unit. For cooling, you can use a standard air conditioning unit or a mini split unit that can heat and cool. I prefer mini splits when it is an option.

Keeping bugs and roaches out of a glamping tent can pose a challenge. Back in the day, you may have relied on a screen porch. More updated technology features a tongue-and-groove floor system that is completely sealed underneath. The tent walls are also secured and sealed to the structure. Additionally, many glamping tents are raised off the ground on a platform that is anywhere from six inches to several feet tall. The only way for bugs, rodents, critters, or anything else to enter is the doorway. With the addition of bug nets, your guests can enjoy the open air without getting eaten alive by mosquitoes or flies.

Now for a technical question that not everyone thinks about: Do I need a permit to build a glamping site with tents? The short answer is, it depends on your location. In some metro areas, tents are only allowed as seasonal dwellings. This means you can rent a tent out year-round, but you must shut it down every so often. However, if you drive fifteen minutes out of the city limits, you may find totally different rules. You may not need a permit to put up a tent there.

Reach out to your local authorities, tell them what you plan on doing, and follow their advice. Yes, you will need a permit in some areas. But if you are in the middle of nowhere, you probably won't.

The ideal location for setting up tents would be nice, smooth, flat grassland. But that is not always possible. Some places require you to build a platform for your tents. I've seen tents put on mountainsides, trees, and water. Great care should be taken for guest safety no matter what platform you choose.

Sometimes a deck framework with tongue-and-groove flooring supports the tent. Because there is no concrete involved, decks are more temporary and environmentally friendly, but they don't work everywhere. In the Rocky Mountains and in hard, rocky terrains, for example, you may find six-by-sixes and concrete footers with a foundation that is more permanent. Before building a platform for your tents, be sure to do the research on any required permits for your location.

How much should you expect to pay for a tent? This depends on shipping costs and the manufacturer. The prices on the low end can vary from a few hundred to a couple thousand dollars. I've seen more rugged tents start around $2,000 and cost as much as $50,000 for the extravagant models. With such a wide range of prices and options, you should add this to the list of things to research for your glamping operation.

Chapter 11
OFFERING AMENITIES

You're going to see a wide variety of amenities, depending on where you camp. If you're traveling across the interstate from one stop to the next, your simple stop might not have much more than a great bathhouse. But if you want to camp at a park for several days, you'll probably see swimming pools, jump pads, and playgrounds. And if you move up to a resort-style property, you will likely see things like miniature golf, petting zoos, obstacle courses, laser tags, and water parks. There's really no limit on what you can do with amenities in resort-style properties.

Bathhouse

As a rule, properties located near a tourist town will not have as many amenities as those built to entertain customers. However, you could still include a couple of bathhouses, so let's explore that option.

When constructing an RV park, cities and communities may have different codes and requirements for bathhouses. It is important to follow NFPA 1194 guidelines as well as the guidelines set out by the city planning and zoning departments.

As you travel and stop at different campsites, you will see a wide range of bathhouses. Some will be stalls similar to a high school locker room, some may be like college dorms, and others will be high end.

Most are middle of the road. Bathhouses should be nice, tiled, clean, and exactly what people need. When it comes to reviews, people really like the option of having individual bathrooms. Dorm-style shower stalls are not as private. If you're planning on charging a higher rate, plan for greater privacy.

With bathhouses and bathrooms, you will see a wide variety of arrangements. I chose to make bathhouses separate for men and women, but bathrooms are unisex. Bathhouses are separate facilities and seldom have waiting lines, but this is not true for bathrooms. I decided it would be much more efficient to make all bathrooms unisex versus having separate male and female restrooms.

Laundry

Your laundry room shouldn't be as much a side hustle as it is an amenity for your property. I didn't realize its true potential until COVID happened. Laundry rooms in a campground are usually quite small. With such close proximity between guests, we had to close the laundry room down. At the time, I thought, *Okay, this is a short-term park. How many people will really be doing laundry during their three- or four-day stay?* Quite a few, as it turns out. We had tons of complaints and even some bad reviews because people were angry that the laundry rooms were closed.

The laundry room can bring in thousands of dollars a week (hundreds for smaller parks), and it will be used by both short- and long-term guests. Long-term guests will spend more money in your laundry room than short-term guests, but either way, it's a nice offering and a moneymaker.

Pool

Any short-term property where people stay for more than a day should have some form of water feature, whether it's a pool, a splash pad, or an elaborate water park. Some properties have two pools because the pools are a little bit smaller, but any pool will require extra daily maintenance.

People often ask whether our pools are heated. I have seen plenty of parks with heated and unheated pools. The value of heated pools will depend a lot on your geographic region and what your customers will expect based on other parks in the area. When your pool opens and closes may also depend on whether it is heated. So, unless you have a heated pool, its season will be very weather dependent, typically beginning at the end of April or early May and ending sometime in October.

When it comes to maintenance and the daily requirements for operating your pool, you will want to check your area's regulations. Some locations require lifeguards, but you can probably build your pool or buy a property with a pool that will not require a lifeguard. The Americans with Disabilities Act requires you to have a handicap lift for your pool.[7] There may be other local laws that govern how you operate your pool. For example, some areas of the country require a pool operator to be certified. To be a certified pool operator, you must take a course and get certified through the state.

Maintaining your pool will depend on whether you have a saltwater or chlorine pool. These have two completely different maintenance requirements. For example, a chlorine pool will need a maintenance team to use a test kit to check pH levels, then add the chemicals needed so the pool can be safely opened. The team will also check throughout the day to make sure the chemical levels are sufficient for the number of users and the amount of chemicals that are lost.

Saltwater pools are uncommon at RV parks, and the maintenance requirements are more involved. I would recommend consulting someone before choosing a saltwater pool over a chlorine pool. Some negatives to choosing a saltwater pool include the up-front costs, as well as the longer amount of time it takes saltwater to kill pathogens in the pool.

We typically close our pools around 9:00 p.m., and we check the levels again to see if any shock treatment or water should be added overnight. Almost every day, we add water because some evaporates and some splashes out. If the pool water gets too low, the water pump can strain and possibly burn out. This leads to pool closures and upset guests.

To avoid this, I highly recommend following a written daily schedule for your pool maintenance. Depending on the level of trust you have in your maintenance team, you might want the manager to make sure it's done correctly. The manager should also be trained in pool maintenance in case someone calls in sick or quits. There should always be someone on site who knows how to maintain your pools.

---

7   "ADA Requirements: Accessible Means of Entry and Exit," ADA.gov, U.S. Department of Justice, Civil Rights Division, February 28, 2020, https://www.ada.gov/resources/accessible-pools-requirements/#:~:text=Large%20pools%20must%20have%20two,of%20exceptions%20to%20the%20requirements.

Splash Pad

One of my properties doesn't have a pool, but it does have a great splash pad. When you're producing marketing materials and looking for ratings from companies like Good Sam, a splash pad will still count as the requisite water feature, and lots of families with smaller children prefer this over a pool anyway.

You'll undoubtedly see properties that have big, elaborate water parks that include a pool and a splash pad. What you can add to your park depends on how much space you have and who your target market is. Water features will also determine how much you can charge per night. I recommend putting a lot of thought into what amenities you ultimately decide to offer. If you do things right, even if your park doesn't have a big, commercial water park, it will be obvious that someone spent tens of thousands of dollars on its design and construction.

Playground

One of the bare minimum amenities that should be available in any campground or RV park is a playground. These come in a wide variety of price ranges. A basic playground will cost around $2,000, but larger commercial playgrounds can cost as much as $50,000–$100,000.

Jump Pad

Another common amenity in family parks is an inflatable jump pad or jump pillow. Not all insurance companies will insure a jump pad on your property, because it can be a huge liability. Jump pads will require a camera that should be staffed and monitored whenever the jump pad is running. This can be a little pricey, so make sure that the jump pad is protected and taken care of properly. I have a jump pad at one of my parks, and to prevent injuries during the hours it is closed, I have a maintenance team inflate it in the morning and deflate it in the evening.

Dog Park

RV owners love their pets, so one of the most important features that you can have for pet-loving campers is a well-designed dog park. A dog park doesn't have to be huge, but it does need a couple things. First, you should offer bags and somewhere to put pet waste. If you don't, your staff will be cleaning up messes constantly. You also want to add a shaded area and somewhere for the guests to sit. Any type of bench will work. It's also common in a dog park to see a separation between a small dog area and a large dog area.

Wi-Fi

Wi-Fi is very important, and it's not considered an amenity anymore; it's a utility and will affect whether people are willing to stay at your property. For this reason, it's imperative to have broadband Wi-Fi.

You have the option of providing a basic Wi-Fi service that everyone can access or an upgraded service for customers who are willing to pay extra. Some parks make a great amount of money charging extra for Wi-Fi; if you do that, it better be really great, or you'll be dealing with complaints all day long.

The guests with high expectations are those who are working remotely or who have children doing homework on the road. Interruptions and poor Wi-Fi are unacceptable, particularly if they paid extra for it. Other guests with high demands are those expecting to stream TV shows and movies while on the road. They want their Netflix, HBO, Hulu, and other streaming services to be as clear as what they have at home. For all these reasons, if you choose to charge for Wi-Fi, you had better deliver amazing Wi-Fi.

The Case for Providing Wi-Fi

A vast majority of today's RV parks lose one out of five stars because of poor Wi-Fi, which directly translates into lost revenue. People make their decisions on where to camp based on ratings, and many people expect and rely on broadband internet access.

I recently upgraded the Wi-Fi at one of my properties. Quotes were anywhere between $50,000 and $90,000, and this simply was not in my budget for the property I was upgrading. So we decided to install the Wi-Fi ourselves.

I'll state the obvious and acknowledge that not everybody can do this themselves. Fortunately, we have a person on our maintenance team who is very knowledgeable about Wi-Fi, and he was able to install it for about $25,000.

From experience, I'll tell you it is best to install Wi-Fi at both your office and your pool area, which can bring coverage to the entire park. Your Wi-Fi service needs to cover all the accommodations where your customers will be staying.

The Federal Communications Commission's definition of basic broadband is 25 megabits per second (Mbps) for downloads and 3 Mbps for uploads. Ideally, you will need closer to 25 Mbps for download and 25 Mbps for uploads; some of today's customers expect even higher speeds that require a fiber-optic connection. These speeds are required for synchronous gaming. Even if you can't afford speeds this high, the Wi-Fi should be reliable, even during peak hours, whether you have two, three, or five hundred customers trying to stream Netflix on their devices.

We expect the demand for higher internet speeds to continue for many years. We also believe most of the folks who work remotely will continue to do that. This ability to work remotely has fueled massive growth in the RV industry over the past few years. This growth has also encouraged remote learning for kids who are still in school. Since all these trends are expected to continue, high-speed broadband internet will continue to be very important.

Installing Broadband Internet and Wi-Fi

By now you've concluded you must have broadband. Now, how can you deliver it? A delivery system is divided into two different components. The first is called backhaul. This refers to the side of the network that communicates with the global internet using an internet exchange point. Backhaul is about 20 percent of the overall engineering challenge of delivering fast broadband speeds. Currently, there are two common backhaul types. One is DSL (digital subscriber line). This technology provides high-speed internet access over phone lines. The other is a cable modem. A modem is a device that uses a coaxial cable connection to deliver an ISP (internet service provider), such as Xfinity. The modem downloads the signal from your ISP and translates it for your local devices, and vice versa. There are other backhaul technologies that provide dedicated internet access, including dial-up, wireless, satellite, and cellular.

Let's expand more on backhaul types. Let's say you've got dedicated internet access (DIA) that is fiber optic, which is what most large parks will need. You have other options besides fiber optic, such as cable, DSL, satellite, cellular service, and Starlink (which is basically satellite). Keep in mind that when more people are using whatever system you choose, some companies limit the data speed using a data cap. This is especially true from 7:00 p.m. to 9:00 p.m., when everybody is streaming a show on Netflix or HBO. You will want to ask your service provider about that possibility.

This is why I tend to prefer DIA. It delivers high broadband speeds to every guest 24/7, even during peak hours. If you don't include the highest traffic hours, you can save quite a bit of money, and there are also less-expensive options out there. But during evening times on the other technologies, you'll get much lower speeds per user. Speeds will drop to less than one or two Mbps, which is way too slow for peak internet times. The second component of delivering broadband comes down to access. It is very important your RV customers have access to your high-speed internet throughout your property. That can be a huge challenge. It typically requires 5G technology and enterprise-grade equipment. There are many vendors who sell small, business-grade equipment (including companies like Ubiquiti), but I recommend equipment that is enterprise grade—something suitable for a corporation, not a typical home. This level can consistently translate your high-speed internet for your customers. The equipment will require a higher level of engineering that can account for distance, trees, terrain, and so on.

The internet company should also provide enterprise-grade support. It does not benefit you to install the best equipment if your guests are on hold or can't get their issue resolved in a short period of time. If they experience internet problems, they will likely leave the next day and give you a four-star rating. So be sure you have internet support covered with in-house staff or an ironclad contract with your vendor.

Also, network latency is a big issue. Network latency is the amount of time it takes for a data packet to go from one device to another. Fiber-optic internet provides low latency, which is ideal. Some technologies, such as satellites, have high latency; sometimes over one hundred milliseconds. Starlink has tried to solve this by putting their satellites closer to Earth, but currently, nothing compares to fiber-optic cable. It will provide your best synchronous internet connection. Synchronous connections have a guaranteed, easy-to-manage bandwidth service with consistent upload and download speeds. For streaming video and two-way communications on Zoom and for FaceTime, it is critical to install a fiber-optic system. Fiber allows upward of 100,000 customers to use one internet connection, meaning you will never have difficulties with bandwidth on fiber.

Sometimes fiber isn't available to your park, perhaps because it's too expensive to construct. Internet service providers installing fiber at your site may come back to you with an up-front bill of $30,000 to $70,000. We've even seen construction costs as high as $300,000. In those cases, you may consider other technologies such as microwave or long-term evolution, also known as LTE. It is sometimes referred to as 4G LTE and is a standard for wireless data transmission. It allows you to download your favorite music, websites, and video at a fast speed—much faster than the previous standard (3G) allowed. Also, there is something called TV white space, which allows you to penetrate trees. All of these options can bring an internet connection to your park. Each has pros and cons, and you should review your options.

Implementing high-speed internet doesn't come cheaply. You will need to hire support staff (e.g., your internet service provider) who can monitor your system 24/7. And you cannot just go out and buy a bunch of boxes and radios, install them, and expect them to work day in and day out for years. Your equipment must be enterprise-grade (similar to AT&T or Verizon) and monitored for frequency usage, firmware updates, and bug fixes. It must be a living, breathing machine that is monitored and maintained every day.

There are three ways that you make money with a quality broadband system. The first, of course, is you can increase your rates. If you've proved that you have high-quality internet at your park, you're getting five-star ratings, and guests can see the speed test graphs on your website, this will absolutely justify raising your rates. Some parks will raise their rates by a couple of dollars (some as much as $8 per night) when they launch true broadband Wi-Fi throughout the park.

The second (more indirect) way will be an increase in your star ratings. I mentioned earlier that losing even one star out of five will cost you a significant number of bookings, especially when people compare Google ratings. In many cases, customers decide where to book on just a half-star difference. Because of this, high-quality broadband throughout your park really does drive bookings and increases occupancy. I've seen a properly implemented broadband system drive bookings up by 10 to 20 percent, depending on the park.

The third way is to sell the Wi-Fi via service plans within your park. We like to say that a poor Wi-Fi system is an expense, but a quality, enterprise-grade broadband system brings a high ROI. Many parks choose to include broadband as an amenity, and they tack it on to the rates with unlimited devices and no data caps for anybody. That is certainly the trend, and it's what we're seeing in the hospitality indus-try. Even Motel 6 or the smallest hotel allows an unlimited number of devices on their Wi-Fi.

The RV park industry has lagged on this, but we are catching up. A lot of parks now offer two tiers of internet service, much like high-end hotels do. One (typically free) tier allows you to check email and do low-bandwidth online tasks. For video playback, this will typically not be sufficient. In the second, paid tier, guests can opt for high-speed inter-net that is suitable for video playback. What you choose to do depends on the park, the demographics, and the availability of other options, like cellular, and so on.

Consider this example. Let's say that you're adding an extra $205,000 a year to your bottom line (your NOI) based on these three advantages to your broadband Wi-Fi system. Now, let's take an industry-standard cap rate today of about 4 percent. Divide that $205,000 per year by 4 percent. That increases the value for your property by about $1 million. If you ever wish to sell your property, high-speed broadband will con-tribute to the value of the business. With enterprise-grade broadband, you can increase your rates, your star ratings, and occupancy, and even sell Wi-Fi. All these will be direct contributors to your bottom line.

You won't see these advantages with poor Wi-Fi systems. Some parks try to sell substandard Wi-Fi, but customers get wise very quickly and won't stay past the first day. For these reasons, it is critical to have a quality system with an enterprise-grade support staff so people feel like they're supported when they have issues.

To summarize, broadband Wi-Fi has become a requirement from guests today. The demographics have changed significantly, and people expect the Wi-Fi at your park to work as well and as fast as it does at their home or workplace.

Long-Term Parks

When it comes to amenities at a long-term park, some people will simply be looking for a safe, clean, affordable place to live. They will book the cheapest option that checks the boxes.

A property like that may not have any amenities at all, just sites, hookups, and trash pickup. But there are other long-term RV parks (mostly for the long-term, 55-and-older crowd) that have a lot of great amenities. They provide more of a retirement community atmosphere instead of just an affordable place to live.

Furnishings

When you're budgeting for your alternative accommodations, you'll also need to include funds for furniture. If you don't already know it, all furniture is not created equal. People are harder on things when they are on vacation, so you can't buy cheap items and expect them to last. Make sure you've budgeted for commercial-grade or hotel-quality furniture. Maybe you'll want to create a theme, a rustic look, or something more modern. Whatever it is, make sure it flows throughout your property, so your customers don't feel they are jumping around from a little of this to a little of that. This also makes sense for your photography and marketing materials. Guests sometimes stay longer when they like what they see and feel.

I've also noticed that people get really picky about their mattresses, and rightly so. If you don't get a good night's sleep, you're not going to enjoy your stay, especially since you're on vacation. I caution against buying cheap mattresses. I usually buy hotel-quality mattresses to make sure that everybody's having a great experience.

Chapter 12

HOSTING ACTIVITIES AND EVENTS

I t can be fun—and chaotic—to run special activities and events at your park. Every park is different, and so are the types of events you can plan. This is a great opportunity to provide a unique experience for your guests and differentiate your RV park from others. I'll share some of the experiences I've had with events and the reasons why they're something you may want to do at your park.

Themes

Depending on what type of property you own, you might want to have themed weeks. Some examples of this would be Christmas in July or a water weekend with squirt gun wars and pool activities. Perhaps you could host an event with a pirates-and-princesses theme. (Imagine a little kid's birthday party, but on steroids.)

If you don't have a family park, other themes might be appropriate. I've seen 55-and-over parks do some pretty amazing adult Easter egg hunts, as well as pet costume parades and contests at Halloween. Be creative! And keep in mind the type of guest you wish to cater to.

No matter what your theme is, don't do it if you're not willing to go all out. By "all out," I mean your staff needs to be dressed according to the theme, you have activities throughout the day, and you decorate your office and all your main campsite areas. Your property needs to transform into a magical land of whatever the theme is. Otherwise, it's not worth the effort.

I will say that Halloween is a huge thing. A lot of campgrounds use the entire month of October to celebrate Halloween, and it draws people in. They have trick-or-treating every single weekend, haunted trails, themed parades, and even dog costume parties. And campers love it. These parks sell out for October.

The best thing you can do is think about who your target market is, then brainstorm what you can provide to that target market. Jellystone Parks have fifty-two different themes for the entire year, with one theme for every week. There's no reason you can't borrow from that playbook for several weekends a year.

Adults versus Kids

Whether you're catering to children, adults, families, or all of the above, you need to determine the types of activities you can provide. For families, you will probably need different activities that are appropriate for little kids, teenagers, and families to do together. I'll give you some examples.

One of my properties shows a movie every night. At 7:00 p.m., they show a G-rated movie the whole family can enjoy. But the 9:00 p.m. movie is a PG-13 movie that is more entertaining for teenagers and adults. (As stated earlier, make sure you keep licensing requirements in mind when you have events like this.)

Parks that cater to an older crowd might have more potlucks and get-togethers than other types of parks. This could work especially well during the Thanksgiving holiday. Also, ice cream socials work well in the summer when people want to enjoy the sunshine. Pavilions with garage doors can provide shade when needed and climate control when it's too hot.

Depending on what audience your park caters to, you either want to have a wide variety of activities that are appropriate for different ages or focus your activities on the crowd your park draws. For example, in one of my properties, there is a nearby gospel music festival for a couple of weeks, followed by a national quartet convention. Those events bring in an older crowd. When I schedule activities and themes during these weeks, they are dramatically different from family vacation events. The older crowd prefers bingo games, potlucks, and ice cream socials rather than water fights. These are examples of how you can target your activities to your audience.

When you are planning your activity calendar, you will also want to consider your activity costs. My rule of thumb is that if the activity cost is less than a dollar per person, like kids' crafts, it should be included at no additional charge. But if it's an outdoor movie, donut decorating, or a significant separate activity, then an extra charge is justified. For example, we charge $5 per child for a donut-decorating event. During this crowd-pleaser, we bake frozen donuts in a pizza oven. We then set up a giant table for donut decorating that closely resembles what you'd expect at an ice cream social—sprinkles and all. The kids get a kick out of decorating the donuts with icing, cereal, and various other toppings. It brings in a little bit of income, but it's mostly done to enhance the overall experience.

I've also had great success with a couple of other activities worth mentioning. The first is tie-dyeing shirts. You can buy shirts with the name of your location and preferred design printed on them, then have the campers tie-dye them. If you don't want the mess of dye, fabric markers can be used for coloring the shirts. Both are crafty activities that can bring in additional income.

I tend to favor making most of the activities free or, at most, a few dollars. If you have six activities in a day, choose one that will be a paid activity and make the other five activities free. You never want a kid to show up and not be able to participate because they don't have the money or their parents can't afford it. Therefore, it's best to have themed coloring sheets and crayons available even during a paid activity. That way everyone can participate in something.

Coordinator

If you have a full-fledged activity program at your property, you're going to need somebody to staff it. One option for finding an activities staff member would be to hire a teacher who is off for the summer. I once hired a librarian from a local library who read books to and did different activities with children on the weekends. College students can also be great assets. You can also call local churches and see if whoever coordinates vacation Bible school may be interested in helping. Finding a positive, creative, upbeat person who can work with kids can make all the difference in your activities program.

Mascots

One of the most famous RV park franchises (Jellystone) has a mascot. It's Yogi Bear, which is part of Warner Brothers. Those campgrounds have a bear sculpture on site and a store that sells branded items. These parks commonly offer pictures with a staff member dressed as Yogi Bear, cookies and milk with Yogi Bear, T-shirts of Yogi Bear, and a ton of other merchandise, all related to Yogi Bear.

You don't have to own a franchise to mimic the same idea. There is a park in Pennsylvania that chose a moose for a mascot. They purchased a moose costume, and they sell various items, T-shirts, and photographs related to their moose mascot.

I also have a friend who owns a park in Indiana. She doesn't use a mascot costume. Instead, she has a donkey that everyone adores. Kids love feeding the donkey, parents buy T-shirts that feature the donkey, and pretty much everyone wants to take pictures with the donkey. It doesn't have to be a traditional mascot in a suit; your mascot could be an animal on your property that everybody loves.

Events

Many RV properties hold special events. You could bring in a band to perform concerts on weekends, put on a fishing or barbecue contest, or host a chili cook-off. Events like these are best scheduled during your shoulder seasons and not your main season. These events draw in people on weekends that wouldn't have otherwise been busy. You can either sell tickets only to those who are camping, or (depending on the parking space you have available) you can also sell tickets to locals who wish to attend.

There is a wide variety of options for activities and events depending on the type of property you have. If you can handle the additional work, the sky's the limit on the extra money that you can bring in with activities and events.

Chapter 13

INCORPORATING SIDE HUSTLES INTO YOUR RV PARK

To know what side hustles to add to your RV park, be creative and attentive to your customers' needs. Know what they are looking for, what will keep them in your park longer, and what they would spend more money on. Things that get you excited will also make them excited and willing to spend more money.

A couple of my favorite side hustles are my camp store and my laundry room. I love going over the different amounts of things we sell and matching that with what customers like, and the laundry room takes almost no effort and brings in thousands of extra dollars a month.

Store

My camp stores are a small space inside my RV parks. In one year, camp stores bring in around $160,000. This is a nice extra source of income that doesn't require extra staffing because my employees are already in the office (where the store is) doing reservations, checking guests in and out, and answering customer questions. It does take a little bit of extra work to keep the inventory stocked, but we have SOPs (standard operating procedures) and great inventory systems available.

The busiest day of the week for your store will be Sundays. This is when customers are checking out and buying whatever they want before they leave. The office staff print a report showing everything that was sold for the week, make sure we've restocked from our storeroom, and order what we're out of. If this is not done weekly, it will affect our bottom line. Our employees also use calendar alerts to check our store inventory so we don't get behind.

The types of products that do well in your store depend on what type of park you own. When your park is a franchise or caters to families with kids, parents will buy a lot of branded items and souvenirs for their kids. If you're catering to an older crowd, your store will carry a different inventory. Some of our top sellers are s'more kits, roasting kits, and roasting sticks for campfires. Shockingly, rainbow flames that turn campfires all different colors will sell better in one area of your store than another (they are more of an impulse buy). Not all campgrounds can allow campfires due to burn ordinances, but when they do, these products are big moneymakers.

Drinkware and apparel also sell well, as do fishing supplies if your campsite comes with a fishing pond. One of my favorite suppliers for a camp store is Wilcor. Wilcor sells RV supplies, toys, and random knick-knacks. Their products sell surprisingly fast, and I end up reordering them often. This industry-specific supplier makes a big difference in my camp store business.

Most short-term RV parks have some sort of water feature, whether it's a water park, tubing, or swimming pools. In these parks, items like goggles, floatation devices, earplugs, nose plugs, and just about any water toy will sell well. Depending on where you are located, water-related items may be seasonal products. I try to plan ahead and change out sections of the store with each season, so the store is always making money.

Golf Carts

Another great side hustle at an RV park is golf carts. They are usually rented out 100 percent of the time for a couple reasons. Some use them as entertainment and enjoy riding them around the property. Others use them to get from point A to point B. Maybe guests are in their camper, and they want to go see their buddies in the cabins or take all their stuff down to the pool. Whatever the reason, a golf cart is a valuable means of transportation within the park. There will also be some people who bring their own golf carts. My personal recommendation is that you charge a (smaller) fee for those who bring one in.

I don't purchase golf carts for my parks. Instead, I lease them from Club Car, which has a special program for RV park owners. I charge $50/day, and camp guests can rent them through the same portal they use to rent their RV spot. I also have rules that apply, such as no one under 16 is allowed to drive the golf carts, and there are quiet hours when the carts are gas-powered. As I said earlier, make sure anyone who rents or brings in their own golf cart signs a waiver. I've seen people bring in their own carts and have their kids drive them—only to cause damage in the park.

If they bring their own golf cart, get a copy of their insurance policy. Just like RV campers or cars driving through your property, golf carts can do damage. One time somebody brought their own golf cart and let their kids drive it, which was against our policy. They allowed their 12-year-old to drive, who ended up rolling down a hill, getting badly hurt, and damaging someone else's camper. Without insurance information and their signed waiver, I could have been liable for those damages.

Water Rentals

If your property has a lake, river, pond, or any form of water, water rentals are another great source of income. People will rent tubes, kayaks, or actual boats if you're on a lake. This brings in extra income and adds to your customer experience.

Fishing

Fishing is a favorite with campers. So, if you're on a lake or river, or maybe you just have a pond that you stock with fish, make sure to add that to your marketing material. Fishing may bring people to your property. Stock your store with fishing supplies, because your customers will need bait, hooks, bobbers, and fishing line, and those purchases will improve the bottom line on your store sales.

Fishing licenses and regulations will vary by state. On my properties, I don't need to require fishing licenses because the properties are private and the ponds are sufficiently small, so as to avoid regulation. From what I have seen, if you connect to a public lake or larger body of water, you may be forced to obtain fishing licenses. As in all cases, make sure you review your local laws, and provide waivers that have been reviewed by an attorney to limit your liability.

Day Passes

If you have an attractive park that's on a lake or a beach, next to a river with rafting, or near some other feature for people who aren't camping, you can sell day passes. With day passes, you'll need extra parking, but this could be an extra source of revenue from those who want to enjoy the amenities within your park without sleeping there.

Food Services

A lot of short-term RV parks will provide a food service option. For some, it could be as simple as a food truck that comes in. Others host a snack bar, a pizza kitchen, or a full-fledged restaurant. There are even parks with swim-up tiki bars. You can create a full-service offering like my friends in Wisconsin who have a great cantina where food and drinks are served, or you could just provide pizza. Choose the options that serve your clientele best.

I have a property in the middle of a tourist town where there are a ton of food options and entertainment shows in the area, but I also wanted my customers to have in-house food options if they didn't want to leave the property. So I contracted with Hunt Brothers Pizza. They supply frozen crusts and different toppings that can be added. We customize the pizza and run it through the pizza oven, which only takes a couple minutes. With this operation, I have a freshly made pizza that tastes great and took very little effort. Hunt Brothers also checks my inventory, so I don't have to worry about refilling supplies. The profit margins on these pizzas are about $5 each, and we sell a ton of them. We also offer other options that can be run through the pizza oven, like boneless or regular wings.

Whatever food options you decide to offer, this side hustle offers great margins and improves customer satisfaction.

Milk and Cookies

Remember when I mentioned using a mascot? Wouldn't it be great if your mascot could bring milk and cookies to the kids at your site? This could be for a birthday, a holiday, or a special event. I charge $20 per site visit for one child and $5 extra for each additional child (so $25 for two children, $30 for three, and so on.) I have a team member dress up in our mascot costume, and another team member escorts our mascot to the party carrying a picnic basket and delivering prepackaged cookies and small milk cartons (I get these supplies from Sam's Club).

We do this from 6:00 p.m. to 9:00 p.m. because we want to minimize the commitment hours, and we don't want our team member to be dressed in a costume for too long, especially when it's hot. We schedule these for consecutive fifteen-minute time slots, so the mascot doesn't need to change into the costume several times. If your property is only busy on the weekends, you could do this on a Friday or Saturday night, then ramp it up to seven nights a week during peak season. The children love getting a special visit and a treat.

Laundry

I've already covered laundry as an amenity. However, I'll mention it again here because I also classify the laundry room as one of the best side hustles for an RV park. It's a great extra source of revenue that doesn't take a whole lot of effort. You'll have washers and dryers, and they will need quarters or credit cards to operate. All you will do is maintain the machines and have your housekeeping staff do a cleanup once a day. This is an easy way to take in anywhere from a couple hundred dollars to a couple thousand dollars a week, depending on the size of your park.

Storage

If your property has some extra land that hasn't been developed yet, one of the ways you can make money is to use it for RV storage. People can park their campers for a monthly fee, or you can have the manager put it on a site for them. You'll need extra insurance coverage, but this side hustle can bring in over $100,000 a year.

This is a great benefit to those who come a long distance to visit. Not only do they save money by not driving a big truck and pulling a camper, but they're also saving the time and energy of setting up their camper on site. The other thing this service does is encourage them to visit your property more often.

Note that some parks will offer a variation of this, except they'll leave the camper in the primary section of the campground. The problem with that is it prevents that RV site from being rented out to someone else. What I suggest offers the same service but allows you to make extra income without sacrificing valuable, reservable spots in your park.

Ice

Ice is the second-largest seller in my camp stores. I find it best to use a distributor who provides the ice. Some campgrounds bag and sell the ice themselves, but I have never found the profit margins to be high enough to make the effort worthwhile. Most people purchase ten-pound bags, but you could sell two five-pounders if that's your only option. Ten-pound bags seem to be the standard.

Firewood

Firewood is yet another great side hustle for an RV park, and there are a couple reasons I like it. First, it doesn't take much effort on our part to make the income. Second, it's part of the campground atmosphere. Guests like gathering around a campfire, cooking something, or having s'mores. They like building memories around a fire.

Firewood is one of the top sales inside my camp stores. We sell hundreds of bundles of firewood each week. You have a couple options with firewood. You can either buy from a distributor or buy locally. Distributors are more expensive, so I usually buy from a local supplier. You can also purchase a property with acreage and do the cutting and bundling yourself. There are some campgrounds that make a ton of money packaging and bundling firewood to sell to their guests. Whichever option you choose has a lot to do with your staff and what resources are available.

Section III
OPTIMIZING OPERATIONS

Chapter 14

MANAGING YOUR RV PARK TEAM

When I purchased my first investment property more than ten years ago, it was a vastly different scene than it is now. The park was in bankruptcy. It contained only one hundred sites, and almost all the sites were occupied by people permanently living there.

The full-timers paid just $300 a month, which included utilities. Many of these residents had added their own amenities, like mailboxes and external refrigerators. It was an eyesore. In the early days, I wondered what I had gotten myself into.

The campground was also about as basic as they come. There were no extras, like cabins or glamping tents. There were no amenities to upsell. Nearly every part of the park needed a revamp or, in some cases, a teardown.

It was a rough first year. The property didn't make any money, and neither did I.

By year three, we squeaked by with a $300,000 profit, but that didn't include the debt service. So in reality, I took home $78,000—hardly what I had in mind. But I didn't give up. I cleaned up the park and turned it into an outdoor hospitality resort.

Fast forward eight years, and the property was taking in over $2 million in annual revenue. We've come a long way, and the park is literally unrecognizable to those who knew it ten years ago. We will discuss all the hard work that goes into these operational changes throughout this section.

Your Management Style

In Chapter 2, we started to explore the decision to manage the park yourself park or hire a management company. Now that you have your park, it's time to pull the trigger. Here are your two options in greater detail.

Self-Management

Most people choose to manage their own park in some form, but self-management is not for everyone. Fortunately, self-management does not mean you personally spend hours walking through every corner of your property, addressing every problem as you encounter it. Rather, you manage your own team. Although you won't need to walk the length of your park daily, you may want to spend some time learning the ins and outs of your property, especially if you don't have a lot of experience with RV parks. If you already know how to run the various aspects of your park, it will be easier for you to train your manager. If you are new to the industry and have not spent much time camping, you'll want to hire a general manager with experience.

You need someone who knows your park well enough to instruct your staff on how to care for the different areas of your property. Once you learn the lay of the land, you can start training your team. They will need to know the basics of hospitality, such as housekeeping, maintenance, grounds, and customer service. They should also be knowledgeable regarding campers and hookups, as well as the comings and goings of customers.

If you want a successful park, your management team should be a reflection of you. You and your manager will communicate often, and your manager will make daily decisions for your business. Therefore, one of the most important decisions you will make is hiring a manager with core values like yours. If they do not share your values, you likely won't agree on decisions.

The manager should also have a team-oriented mindset. Having a cohesive team drives revenue and efficiency at your property. Because of this, I recommend including your property manager in every hiring and firing decision.

Your ideal manager should also like to get their hands "dirty." Your park office will be your hub for all things, so its manager needs to be intimately involved with customer service and team delegations. From my experience, hands-on managers are far superior to those who spend time in a back office. Hands-on managers see things as they happen; hidden managers just play defense. You want a manager who is so visible that even the guests know them by name.

When you use a general manager, you will also need a backup plan in case your manager leaves, gets sick, or needs to be replaced. That could mean training one of the other employees as your backup manager or promoting another employee.

Once everyone is trained and your manager can effectively run the park, your job gets a little easier. You can step into the role of overseeing operations, which allows you to oversee from afar and start multiplying your investment into other facilities.

This is the exact path I have taken. At present, I manage my managers from a distance. I can do this efficiently and skillfully because I spent years on site learning all that I needed to know about the property.

I visit each property for a couple of weeks each year. This allows me to have a more thorough check-in with the staff regarding campground needs as we prepare for the next season. I try to pair my visits with new staff trainings and simultaneously take care of the maintenance required for the end of a season.

Of course, this is just my management style; you don't have to manage your team the same way. But I will say that these in-person visits help me make better decisions for planning out capital expenses and reviewing what operational improvements could be made. I also sense that the staff feels a greater connection to me and our mutual goals when I make it a priority to visit, allowing us to work better together.

Hiring a Management Company

If you are less confident, have very little time, or feel that self-management may be too stressful, you may look into a second option: hiring a management company. These folks will take care of the tasks mentioned above, including maintenance, daily operations, and park preparations for each season. Using a management company allows you to maintain your business while not having to operate the park. Some management companies also help grow your park by assisting with reservation systems, marketing, and web design. All these services can justify hiring a management company, but it comes with a higher price tag.

I've also found that management companies have more of a cookie-cutter approach that isn't as customizable as you might want. In most cases, you will probably feel more removed from the organization and operations of your property than you would if you managed the business yourself. You won't feel as intimately familiar with each asset at the park, and you won't get firsthand knowledge of when upgrades and maintenance are needed or what park guests are saying in casual conversations around the park.

Another factor impacting your management decisions is the size of your park. If you have a very large park, a management company may make it easier to operate. Smaller parks, like mom-and-pop parks, are easier to tackle by yourself, so you can forgo the expenses of a management company.

In the beginning, you will likely end up managing your park on some level. The rest of this chapter will focus mainly on self-management, but all these elements are important for your business to succeed. So even if you plan to outsource to a management company, make sure you read these sections thoroughly.

Types of Employees

In addition to your general manager, you will need to hire a team. There are a few ways to find your team. You can send out ads, hire work campers, or search for students.

Traditional Hiring

The traditional hiring method is to send out ads and hire locals. Some park owners choose this route, and hiring locals has multiple benefits. Local employees may be more familiar with the area, know the culture and history of the area, and may even be knowledgeable about the property. Locals are the most likely hires to be stable, year-round employees, but they may not be as experienced with RVs, camping, and park duties.

Hiring Work Campers

Another option is to hire a work camper—someone who lives in a camper and travels around the country, working at different parks for different seasons. They may work up north in the summer months and move south for winter. Their movement often depends on weather and a park's open seasons, as many parks are not open all year. If your park is not open year-round, you may consider work campers for seasonal employment.

Work campers are typically used to working for a lower wage in exchange for a free site to park their camper (or a discounted rate). When determining their lodging arrangements on the property, be careful, because you can get in trouble with accounting. A lot of work campers are people in retirement who turn to camping for the opportunity to travel and earn some wages to support their retired lifestyle. Most of them will have had two or three careers by this point, so you'll often find that work campers come with a wide variety of skills. Work campers may have been contractors, accountants, or plumbers previously. Others become work campers because they need money in retirement to cover medical expenses.

Hiring work campers comes with pros and cons. For one, these workers live nomadically and are less likely to have a lot of other commitments interfering with work. This gives them time to help manage your property. Another pro is their work experience. Since most are retirees, they've had experience with many jobs and may have skills that fit the park's needs.

On the other hand, with retirement often comes a more leisurely lifestyle. Some may not have as much energy or motivation as you want in an employee. Their commitment to your park can depend on their position and your expectations of their work. Also, since they enjoy traveling, some work campers may only be with you for one season, then try another park in the area the next time that season comes. In other words, their employment is less stable, and you may need to keep finding or recruiting new work campers.

I have struggled to hire a property manager who is a work camper. For managers, I need someone with more experience and motivation, and I need them to be looking for a long-term position. Nevertheless, there are certainly some types of parks that thrive with work campers as managers. Typically, long-term parks offer good jobs for work campers, whereas the fast-paced environment of outdoor hospitality parks can be more exhausting for them and you.

Hiring Students

A third method for building a team is to hire students. These can be J-1 (foreign visa) students or locals in high school or college. All can make great hires but may not be long-term employees. Each group has similar schedules and work needs, with the most availability in the summer. If your park is seasonal and open only in the summer, this group might be just what you want. Let's discuss each group briefly.

J-1 students come from other countries seeking employment or a place to study in the United States. They are on work or student visas and need a place to stay. That means you will likely have to provide lodging for them if they work for you. This is more convenient for RV parks with lodge buildings already on the property. J-1 students can work and temporarily live on the property, perhaps with quicker training because they are on the scene more.

High school students are another option. They are typically looking for a summer job and short-term employment. College students would be similar applicants. They may be interning through their college or just hoping for a summer employment opportunity. I have used students for internship programs, which has been excellent. In fact, one of the best employees I had was an intern for a couple of seasons. He had experience with the camping industry, he was a marketing student at a university, and he was an Eagle Scout. He worked on multiple projects, including activities for our social media, email marketing, and many other things that I would otherwise forget to do.

There are plenty of options for hiring staff for your campground. Of course, you can use a mix of hiring methods to fill open positions. Whether you hire work campers or locals, I recommend hiring your manager from within when it is an option. Choose someone with more permanent or long-term employment plans at your park.

Job Descriptions

When you hire your staff members, have their roles well defined. Make sure that they understand exactly what you expect of them. Creating job descriptions that are very specific is a good place to start. Some of the most important job duties will be those of your manager. They will have a lot on their plate and will have some authority over the work of other staff members. Keep job descriptions on file for quick and easy reference. When new employees are hired, the job descriptions can serve as a walk-through of the skills needed and duties to perform. We will detail the different jobs and tasks at an RV park later in this section, but note that some tasks can be shifted around to different roles at the park.

Make your job descriptions specific and ensure that they represent legal and fair jobs. Also, check that your descriptions are not discriminatory. I've hired some outstanding female maintenance employees, and I've had outstanding male housekeepers (so I don't call them "maids"). Similarly, I've hired work campers who are often husband/wife teams.

I've found that by carefully thinking through your descriptions, you can minimize the chance of being discriminatory in your wording.

Fair and Equitable Pay

When making hiring decisions and creating job descriptions, you will need to determine the appropriate pay for each position. I'll start the conversation for you by discussing the general pay ranges.

Keep in mind that the two largest determining factors for pay are the location of your park and what you expect from your staff members. Your managers will receive the highest pay of those on site, but I have seen a wide range of pay for management positions. Some park owners pay their managers as little as $40,000 per year, and others pay as much as $75,000 per year. A manager's housing may even be included in their compensation. But in these cases, the alternative compensation—such as in the form of discounted or "free" housing—must be reported to the IRS as a benefit. Make sure you consult an accountant or tax lawyer when you set up these unique scenarios.

If you have a small, long-term site, it is very possible that your staff's pay will take the form of a reduced rate on their rent. In these situations, the park may not need full-time employees, or the park needs can be handled during only a few hours a day. In contrast, if you own a massive outdoor hospitality resort, the manager's pay will likely be on the $75,000-per-year end of the spectrum. At such large parks, staff members will need a lot of different skill sets. On top of the wide range of skills required, your manager will be working many more hours, so it makes sense that their wages will be higher. They may even receive some kind of bonus or commission based on performance.

Outside of management, staff members typically work at an hourly rate. They're also likely to earn holiday pay since the parks are very busy during the holidays, such as Independence Day, Memorial Day, Labor Day, and even Christmas. Because these employees are working holidays, I'm of the opinion that they should get a bonus.

You may also consider having contracts with built-in incentives. Some owners have been successful in implementing a contract with bonuses for items like showing up on time, working the entire duration of their shift, and not calling in sick. Allowing hardworking employees to have some extra compensation at the end of the year can motivate them to follow these guidelines.

Training

You will need to train your team. And if your park runs seasonally, you will be training employees often. I like to visit my parks at the beginning of each season and assist with my teams' preparations. I believe this gives my parks the best chances of being successful and operating in a way I intend. If this sounds grueling and miserable to you, it's not a necessity. You can have your property manager train staff members at the beginning of each season.

Even with the best-laid plans, you will likely need to continue hiring throughout the season. Sometimes people get sick, or perhaps someone was not the best fit. In a best-case scenario, your park has taken off with more customers than expected, leaving you needing extra hands.

When surprises like this come up, the question then is, How do you train them? One way I address this ongoing need is to have team leads or managers for each department who can train new hires. You could even use someone who has been at the property for a long time and knows the ins and outs as a buddy for new employees to come to with questions. Having this mentor allows managers to continue training and work without continuous question or interruptions. The buddy helps train the new staff, shows them around the property, and helps them feel comfortable. Using the buddy system also builds a more functional team overall.

Scheduling

Scheduling is one of the most essential parts of your business because it controls your payroll. Your payroll will be one of your highest expenses, if not the highest expense. Employee hours will depend on how busy you are. For instance, if a lot of guests check in on Fridays, you should ensure that you have a large enough team to shoulder the load, which often means longer hours and more staff members working the park on those days. Similarly, if the bulk of your guests tend to check out on Sundays, you will need more employees working housekeeping on Sundays and perhaps Mondays.

I like to look ahead at reservations for the upcoming weeks and then schedule my staff members accordingly. While planning, I ensure that if more guests show up than planned, I will still have enough staff working the grounds.

You'll want to allot employees for tasks inside and outside the office to support what is needed at the time. This comes with the caveat that you'll need to make sure the office hours match up. For example, if you have somebody scheduled to be in the office until 8:00 p.m. and no one outside the office to help guests, the office employee must shut down the office to assist guests. Otherwise, the guest in need of help will become upset and likely not return to your park, nor recommend your park to others.

However, if the office is shut down to help another guest, new guests may arrive and be disappointed in your customer service and leave before checking in or leave bad reviews. These two examples illustrate the importance of scheduling properly to cover all of your park's and customers' needs.

Turning back to the subject of hiring campers, it's often best to hire a couple rather than an individual. You are giving up a site so your work campers can be there, so it's best to maximize how many employees live at one site. If you hire an individual, you won't get as much labor out of the work camper site.

However, hiring a couple can make scheduling difficult. Often, a couple will request time off together. When running a small operation, giving them the same days and times off each week is tough. Include this as a consideration when building your team.

You may also find an app or program that helps you and your staff agree upon schedules that work best. There are a ton of great software and apps for scheduling, and which one works best depends on what type of staff you have. For example, if you staff your park with seasonal high school students, they will likely be able to use technology in order to access and alter their schedule in a sophisticated format. However, you may encounter employees who are not as tech savvy, which means you might need to print out schedules instead. The preferences of your staff members will impact your scheduling methods. Furthermore, because scheduling affects your payroll, you can either continue doing the scheduling yourself or have one of your managers operate the schedule to fit a labor budget you provide.

Scheduling differs for every property and type, especially if you have a long-term park. If the park is small enough, a general manager and a maintenance manager are all you need. For a short-term property, you may have an entirely seasonal workforce. In any case, personal choice will also play a role in scheduling. You want to pick the least time-consuming scheduling method that works for you and your business.

Taking Breaks

When you are scheduling, you are required by law to allow break times for staff members. They will need a lunch break and a few fifteen-minute breaks. Every state has different requirements, so make sure you know what these requirements are. Check with your state's Department of Labor (or similar agency) to make sure you are compliant.

Schedule breaks so that there are people working in the park at all times. You don't want anyone on break during peak check-in hours.

Scheduling breaks also allows your employees to know ahead of time when they will need to finish the task they are working on. For instance, it's inconvenient to have housekeepers take a break when they are half done with turnovers, because they could get behind on time-sensitive duties. And you will want your managers to work without wasting time thinking about when they should break; they need to focus on all the tasks that must be done before break time.

Enable Employees

When you run across teaching moments where you feel that the employee could have made a better decision, it's more effective in the long run to give them an opportunity to try a solution themselves first. They were enabled with your permission to try a solution, and they witnessed how their decisions played out. Now you have their attention when you discuss more effective solutions together. The result of this is an employee actively thinking, *What decision could I make that would be best for the park?* In other words, you have a rock star.

This applies to park maintenance as well. Create a high-level schedule of park maintenance tasks, but allow your maintenance team to have ownership in how to carry out these tasks to ensure optimal results. Do certain amenities or assets fail more than they should? Ask your team what they believe would make a difference—let them to create a plan that addresses the issue. Not only will your operations run more smoothly, but your park's value will also increase, and you won't spend your entire season playing defense.

Promotions

If you have staff members who stay on for an extended amount of time and prove themselves to be hard workers, you will likely want to promote them. My last two property managers came from my team. Both ladies worked their way from housekeepers to housekeeping managers to property managers. Jobs don't need to be exclusive. If an employee starts as a housekeeper, they can move up to property management if they demonstrate the skills necessary to operate in that position. It is always important to see somebody's work ethic before hiring them for a higher position that is crucial to your business. Promoting from within your ranks allows the employee to become familiar with your park and how things operate before they receive additional responsibility.

For smaller operations, it is imperative that everyone on your team, including the manager, is willing to jump in and help wherever they are needed. A manager who was promoted from your staff will find it easier to help in multiple areas of the park. If you hire someone who was a general hotel manager, they are unlikely to willingly clean a cabin when somebody calls for housekeeping.

When I first started, I hired people with primary and secondary roles, so there was always someone who could serve as a backup for a different position. For example, I hired a housekeeper who was a backup for activities and a maintenance person who could work in the office during busy check-in and check-out times. Whatever jobs you give your staff members, they should be comfortable and skilled at them. For instance, an activities position may not be best for someone shy or uncomfortable with children. You need a well-trained, versatile team able to help with multiple aspects of the park.

Chapter 15

DEVELOPING YOUR RESERVATION SYSTEM

You will need to know the basics of reservations to operate your park business successfully. There is a lot more that goes into reservations than just collecting payments. In fact, there are numerous techniques to maximize your revenue before guests even step foot in your park. This section will cover some important strategies for making the most of reservations, including the software you use, dynamic pricing, optimizing sites, hosting groups, handling cancellations, and screening tenants. With your hard-earned dollars at stake, you'll want confidence in how reservations work for both long- and short-term parks.

Software

To make your business run smoothly, you'll want to use some type of software for reservations. It's important that you choose a method that works best for your park. You will find some mom-and-pop-run properties that are still doing things on paper, but that isn't the most efficient way to run your business. Even if you run a long-term park where you have fewer changes in reservations, you still need software, especially for a larger park.

For short-term parks, there is no question about it—you need an operating software system to assist with multiple tasks. Your software will help optimize your occupancy, manage your rates, file reports, and even complete some of your accounting. It will also be your point-of-sale (POS) system for your store (if you have one) and will aid you with ordering inventory.

Since you will use your software for these many important tasks, you'll want an intuitive system. Choose a solution that performs tasks efficiently and without complicated interactions with your staff. You don't want software that requires numerous steps and commands from your team or one that takes weeks to train staff on how to operate it. Not only will that be inconvenient, but you will also be using up labor hours. Plus, it will be even harder for a staff member who joins in the middle of the season. You don't want them stumbling through their work during weeks of high business. I did not understand the importance of selecting good software until the one I used forced my staff and me to spend weeks in training.

Today, I use Campspot, which I chose after reviewing various software options. I managed to increase my income by 50 percent after switching to their software because of the features they offer that make a business function smoothly. Campspot provides tools for dynamic pricing, lock fees, and site optimization. It's great for my short-term park operations.

When it comes to software for a long-term park, the needs will be very different. You won't need all the extra functions you would at a short-term park. You only want a system to keep track of your tenants, when rent payments are due, whether to apply late fees, and how long leases are. The needs would be similar to those of a mobile home park or a multifamily property. One system I like is Buildium, which I use for more than just my long-term parks. I find Buildium useful for my mobile home parks and small multifamily properties as well.

Like other options, it can do much more than the general landowner's rental duties just mentioned. So if you have other similar properties, you may be able to use your existing software to manage your RV park as well. If you don't currently use software and you own a super small park, you can probably get away with using an Excel spreadsheet. However, this option eliminates your ability to make reservations online, which means you could lose a huge customer base.

Pricing

When setting your general pricing for the campground, I believe it is important to look at a number of factors. One of the most relevant factors is neighboring parks—if there are any nearby. Consider what they are charging for overnights and weekly guests, and whether they offer more or fewer amenities. You also want to consider the general feel of the comparable campgrounds and whether guests are piled in or spaced out with plenty of green space or trees between them. Campers will often pay more for privacy and the feeling of not being "on top of" a neighboring RV.

I also look at the proximity of the park to desirable attractions. Is your park closer to a local attraction? That can factor in to a higher cost. Also, what is the local demand versus availability? If neighboring parks and alternative housing are nearly always booked, you can demand a higher price.

Another comparable is whether there are nearby state or national parks. If so, what are they charging? Keep in mind that state and national parks nearly always lack in their amenities compared to private parks, so this price will typically be much lower than what you can ask for in your own park. But it can serve as a guideline.

Finally, there are some less-influential factors, such as what local hotels might be charging (they are indirect competitors) and what a comparable market might charge. For example, I would consider Branson, Missouri, a market that is comparable to Pigeon Forge, Tennessee. They tend to draw similar clientele for similar reasons.

Dynamic Pricing

A great feature of the software program I use is dynamic pricing. Even if you don't recognize the term, you are likely familiar with the concept of dynamic pricing, as hotels, airlines, gas stations, and other businesses have used it for years. When you book a hotel room on a holiday weekend in a touristy town, you will pay a much higher rate than you would if you booked one for a random Tuesday in a less-popular city. Or, if you decide to book a flight the day of rather than six months in advance, you may be booking one of the last seats available, which will be more expensive. These prices are dynamic, meaning they change based on a variety of factors.

You have the right to use dynamic pricing at your park. Different software companies manage pricing differently, and some allow you to decide how prices change. Before changing prices, I recommend you take advice from the software companies. Some of them have data scientists who can inform you of the dynamics that work best.

Dynamic pricing won't be a topic of much discussion or knowledge among those in the camping industry. When I first started using dynamic pricing, it wasn't a commonly used technique among RV parks. I ended up picking random rates and seeing how they worked. My rates increased 10 percent for every 10 percent increase in occupancy after the park reached 50 percent occupancy. To illustrate, say my base rate was $50 per night. Once my property reached half full, that $50 increased to $55, to $60.50, to $66.55, and so on as the park booked out.

Of course, you do not have to use this same strategy. You can find whatever prices work for your park. You can offer flat fees, but I highly suggest you consider dynamic pricing, even if you only use it to increase prices by a small percentage. It can really help you get the most out of your rental profits, especially if you choose to raise prices during holidays, like New Year's, when extra profit can provide employee bonuses.

Occupancy Optimization

Occupancy optimization is another way to maximize profits. You want to ensure that you're optimizing all the sites you have at the highest capacity possible. That is extra important for seasonal properties because you only have certain dates to bring in all your income for the year.

Modern software programs are very helpful in organizing occupancy at your park. Before this digital innovation, you'd feel like you were playing Tetris to optimize your park. You'd have a grid with the properties listed in a column and the dates across the top. When people reserved sites and times that overlapped with others, you would lose income for however many nights you could not book one group. Then you would rearrange to match the reservations. This means you could lose thousands of dollars—and tens of thousands in larger parks—for not optimizing your park reservations.

The latest software programs will increase your bottom line and save you hours of time.

Thankfully, new software options can win a game of RV park Tetris within seconds of receiving reservations. Your software ensures that you have the highest occupancy possible at your park. However, some campers are accustomed to choosing their site within the park. If you allow them to do so, they stop the software from moving reservations around and maximizing occupancy. To balance occupancy rates and customer choice, some parks use a lock fee to help control the options. If somebody wants to choose a specific site, they can pay extra to lock in their preference. However, this can create a problem if your property is popular and has a high occupancy. The use of these lock fees also means you can't move a camper to a new location, so your income may not be optimized, as you could lose out on an additional reservation.

I was hesitant, to say the least, when Campspot encouraged me to try out a lock fee. I didn't want to lose a ton of money by letting people choose their sites, but I reconsidered and gave it a try. I had to decide on the price, and I ended up asking for an extra $100 for those who wanted to choose their site (note that $15–$20 is a more standard fee). After the first year of the experiment, I reviewed my numbers and found that the property took in $20,000 extra in lock fees. Although that sounds like a significant amount of money, you must realize that you're often losing money due to a less-optimized occupancy rate. That $100 lock fee is only equal to one or two nights, depending on your site availability. If the customers block that site out for a week, you're losing money. If you choose to use lock fees and allow customers to select their sites, plan carefully how much you want customers to pay so that you aren't losing money. If you choose not to allow people to choose their site, have some thorough answers on your frequently asked questions page so your office can still provide great customer service.

Another bonus to software is that most programs allow your customers to request add-ons (such as a golf cart rental, s'mores ingredients, or firewood) when they make the reservation over the phone or online. You can use dynamic pricing on these too. You will have to determine which of the many opportunities to increase your revenue will suit your property and business. Make sure you are methodical when choosing your software, and unless your operation is very small, don't go without one.

Groups, Clubs, and Events

A third method to increase reservations is hosting groups, rallies, and special events. What you can offer will be very specific to your property and location, but you will need one thing to host any of the above: a meeting area. A pavilion or conference room that can host a large group of people would do the trick. Bear in mind that although you can bring in some extra profits by hosting groups and rallies, they have their downsides.

The parties allow you to fill many of your sites. Unfortunately, most want to book your park during your busiest months, like June and July. On top of that, they usually want a discount. For that reason, if you are operating at high occupancy during the requested time, I suggest declining group reservations through your peak seasons. Otherwise, you sacrifice the ability to fill those sites with regular business. That also means that if the group decides to cancel, you will lose the income necessary for your park to remain open during your less-busy seasons.

One way to get around this risk is by offering a different cancellation policy for groups, especially for those booking during peak seasons. You'll want to make it difficult to cancel without significant penalties. They won't like that policy, but that's okay, because you can sell those sites to an individual camper who will pay full price anyway.

Second, hosting groups can be disruptive to your other guests. If the groups only rent out half of your park, you will still have other customers dealing with the large group's gathering. They may be noisy or take up your cookout areas at inconvenient times. Customers may complain even if the groups aren't doing anything out of the ordinary. It's like a crowd at a restaurant: Even if those at the crowded table are doing the same things you are, they are causing significantly more noise than your smaller party. Because of this, your other guests may leave bad reviews and not return to your park, even if the group did nothing wrong.

On a related note, sometimes the large groups take up more space than they intend. It can be hard to control such large groups. Consider trying to control the group at your park's swimming pool. If half of your customers decide to go swimming together, your pool will be significantly busier than usual. The remainder of your guests would feel overwhelmed by the number of people in one area. You can create multiple solutions to this if you find it necessary. For example, you could set limits on how long groups can take up a public space, like five hours for a cookout. You could include a note when other guests are reserving spots to inform them that a large group will also be staying at the park. You could include reservations for certain public spaces on your property. In any case, you will want to have a system set up that doesn't cause you to lose money or your other guests to get upset.

Up-Front Payments and Cancellations

We already discussed a way to prevent big groups from canceling, but that still leaves the possibility that individuals and small groups will cancel. Sometimes things come up last minute, and guests want to change their reservation plans. To deter this, you must decide how much your customers must pay up front. The RV park industry is moving toward 100 percent up-front payments for reservations (which I also do), although you can still find parks that don't require anything. Some may require 50 percent up front and allow guests to pay the rest as they arrive.

How you handle cancellations and how much people pay up front are often codependent. You don't want customers to be able to cancel right before they're supposed to come, because you can't just rebook the site on the spot. But you also don't want them to refuse to spend any money because they have to hand you $1,000 before checking in. So you may choose to go for a 50 percent up-front payment for guests to make reservations. If they reserve months in advance, there is always the chance that they will forget they paid $500 up front or will have more money ready to spend once they arrive.

In my experience, the less money that people pay up front, the less likely they are to spend money once they get to your property. They come with a certain amount of money they're willing to spend on vacation to buy food, items from the gift shop, activity extras, and other add-ons we have talked about. If you choose to only allow payments to be made upon arrival, that money will come out of what they planned to spend while they're there.

How does this impact cancellations? How much guests pay up front will impact how much you refund them if they cancel their stay. Other circumstances will also affect refunding and cancellation policies, such as how close to their reservation dates they cancel, whether it is a short- or long-term park, and what the standard procedure is for RV parks near you. The refunded amount may change if a customer cancels within a certain number of days of their scheduled stay. For example, some parks allow for a full refund if guests cancel thirty days or more in advance, then decrease the amount refunded for cancellations under thirty days prior. Others only require seven days' notice for full refunds and offer no refunds for any cancellations closer than seven days. Parks often deduct a small amount from the refund as a cancellation fee, typically between $15 and $25. This fee can depend on what guests have already paid and the money you put into preparing their stay.

Although you can treat cancellations like late-work policies in school, (deducting more from the refunded amount for later cancellations), you can also use two other options. For one, if people cancel inside the late period, you can explain that none of their payment will be refunded.

People may dislike that option, which is when you can present option two: rescheduling their stay. Can you move their stay to a different date? That means more work for you, but with a good software system, you should be able to determine your availability and book them for new dates in a few clicks. I caution you that some customers will try and trick you by using this option to change their reservation dates so that they can cancel them and be refunded. You should have detailed notes in your software to record their transactions, so they can't get around your policy.

Cancellation policies also rely on how long people plan on staying at the park. Short-term parks tend to allow fewer days' notice for full refunds. For my short-term parks, guests must cancel ten days or more before their reservation to receive all their money back, minus the $15 cancellation fee. I have heard of parks that request just forty-eight hours' notice for those canceling a one-day or week-long stay. Long-term parks usually ask customers to make cancellations at least thirty days in advance, which holds true for any who stay for more than a month.

When determining your cancellation policy, I highly recommend you check how other parks in the area handle cancellations. With that information, you can gauge what terms and conditions are beneficial for your park, reasonable for customers, and similar to nearby parks. You do not want cancellation policies that scare away customers, but you also don't want customers to cancel often because it is easy to do so and get a full refund.

Keep in mind that you are going to get some pushback for the cancellation fee no matter the policy, as people like to complain about losing money despite how unreasonable their stance may be. You can do multiple things to deal with those who argue over the fee. First, you should include your cancellation policy on your website. That serves as a reference when people question why they must pay a fee to cancel their stay and allows customers to reserve with the knowledge of what they must do to receive a refund for a cancellation. You should also include this policy in your confirmation email.

Some people won't read the policy, and others will still want a better reason than "it's on the website" or "your confirmation email mentioned it." You can politely explain to them that their reservation costs you money, as does the system you use to grant them a refund. After all, you are not only paying for them to take a site at your park, but you also have staff putting in hours to prepare for their reservation and deal with cancellations. On top of that, you pay for the credit card processing fee.

You don't need to explain all those details to customers, but you can inform them that it costs you money to take, make, and break their reservation. Then, simply apologize and express that the fee portion cannot be refunded.

Tenant Screening and Rent—Long-Term Parks

At long-term parks, you need to perform background checks on all potential tenants. You want to ensure that you are hosting safe, law-abiding people. Some software programs offer background checks as a feature. For example, the Buildium product I use checks criminal histories and provides a credit check for all applicants. It even has a pet-screening feature that verifies whether a pet is legitimately a service animal.

Whatever screening requirements you have must be standard for all potential tenants. In other words, you should treat everyone equally and ask for the same information from them (to avoid accusations of discrimination). You should look for multiple sources confirming the information they give you. For example, if you want proof of income, you want the amount the tenant gives, verification from their employer, and pay stubs. Other things to look at include criminal records, credit scores, and eviction histories. These people are not likely to have perfect credit or squeaky-clean backgrounds, so you must decide on qualification standards and stick to them.

I want my tenants to make at least three times the rent that I require them to pay. They need to be able to pay the rent and still make a living for themselves. I also want tenants who have not been evicted within the last five years. Similarly, my tenants can't have horrible criminal histories. However, I also want to see when they were charged with committing any crimes. If they have been clean for twenty years (and not incarcerated during that period of time), then they may qualify as tenants. You will decide what limits you want for your park and the qualifications you require from your potential clients. Be mindful that they likely won't be without some flaw in their history or finances. You don't want to be so strict that you have no customers, but you also want your park to be as safe as possible. You also want to make sure you don't discriminate; provide the same treatment for everyone.

Once you have your screening standards, you need to set standards for payments, such as how people pay their rent, what they are paying for, and by what dates they need to pay. I typically charge my tenants one month's rent as a deposit. By the end of their tenancy, they will receive their deposits back if they have kept up with their rent and haven't caused any damage to the property. How much you charge for rent will also depend on your utilities and other expenses for their sites. Whatever it costs you for a tenant's space on your property will be the amount you charge them and then some. If you are unsure of your pricing, check out how nearby parks handle rent and screening.

How you handle reservations will depend on your software, your park style, and what is standard procedure in your area. Short-term parks can host a wide range of people, and you want to ensure that you're still making a profit while taking in campers and protected when campers cancel their stay. Long-term parks require more screening on customers setting up camp. In any event, you will need to stay on top of scheduling and payments, so your park can continue to grow and succeed. How you do it all is entirely up to you. You just have to figure out the route you want to take and get the tools necessary. Then, stick to the rules you've created.

Chapter 16
MAKING MARKETING WORK FOR YOU

To make money, you need customers to use your property. To get those customers, you are going to need some industry-specific marketing. Let's talk about the marketing categories you will need.

Website

Today, every business needs a great website. Fortunately, they're not priced astronomically like they used to be. I recommend using an industry-specific marketing company to create the best website possible. Use high-quality photos and videos on your website. They're absolutely worth the investment when it comes to drawing in more guests. You're going to need all the photos and videos that you can possibly get.

You may include sections of your website that cover your amenities, activities, themed weekends, special events, information on the area you are in, "Our Story," a map of the grounds, links to reservations, office hours, phone numbers, email addresses, etc.

Google Ads

One of the biggest ways I drew in my first customers was with Google AdWords (now called Google Ads) and pay-per-click marketing. In general, I have found that properties located in popular areas may not be as easy to market with simple organic search results. This is because there could be thousands of other companies trying to market to these visitors. In this case, I will often turn to paid advertising, in addition to trying to grow my organic SEO value. Truth be told, I utilize Google Ads for every park I own, and the majority of my business is derived from this source of advertising.

Most people are not experts at digital advertising, so I encourage you to use industry-specific marketing teams that can help drive your business. One way they can help is by suggesting search keywords that will direct customers to your website. For example, maybe somebody has searched for "camping near Yosemite." If your park fits that need, you want to make sure that your property will pop up in the search results. For this to happen, you're going to need to make an arrangement with Google. You can also have those teams design the advertisements. A great website with high-quality photos and videos paired with an effective online marketing strategy will start to bring in customers.

Reviews

I encourage park owners to seek reviews—and especially at opportune times. For example, when an employee favorably resolves a guest's issue, I suggest they remind the guest that reviews are always welcomed. We also send emails to guests, thanking them for staying. We will ask for reviews in that email. You could also consider incentivizing your employees to get good reviews by offering bonuses at certain milestones.

Successful RV park owners control their reviews and their online presence. You will want to respond to each review, whether it is positive or negative. In responding, however, it is important to avoid arguing with a reviewer online. You must take these disagreements offline. Even when you're right and the reviewer is wrong, arguing makes you look unprofessional. There are companies that do industry-specific review management, so let's talk a little bit about them.

I used to try to respond to all reviews myself. It was awful and time consuming. During peak season, one property can get five or six reviews a day, depending on the size of the park. As a manager or investor, you do not have time to respond to every review, although that job is important to your success. Here's why.

Think about when you choose to eat at a new restaurant. You'll pull up Google or Yelp to check out what people are saying about it. These reviews are the digital first impression for a business. As a property owner, you essentially have three options for managing reviews:

1. Respond to each review yourself,
2. Have somebody on your team respond, or
3. Use a professional, industry-specific marketing company to reply.

I turned over my review responses to a company three years ago. The company sends nice replies to all positive reviews, which I can see as they happen. I don't require approval for those, so that allows me to get business done and not have to think about it.

In the event there's a negative review, the company will send me a message with their suggested response. I can either approve it or add more to it, which I often do. For example, I had a bad review recently from a customer who was raging mad because, according to them, their cabin didn't have running water. In reality, the water had been turned off for approximately thirty minutes in the middle of the day because of an annual city inspection. This was out of my control, so I made sure that my response included my side of the story and wasn't an argument with the guest.

To do this, I said something like "I apologize for your experience, but the water was only off for about thirty minutes for a city inspection that happens for a short time each year." Omit anything negative about or to the guest, and make sure that the reader knows exactly what happened, so it doesn't impact their decision to stay at your property. Using a company to do that for you is much more efficient than doing this yourself. They will tell you each time one of those reviews come in, whether that's on Google, Yelp, or Tripadvisor. Regardless of your intention to hire a company or reply to reviews yourself, have some system in place to respond appropriately to each review of your property.

Social Media

Social media accounts should be frequently updated, preferably daily. There are so many things you could talk about through social media. To name just a few, you could post about upcoming events at your park or in the area, discounts and specials, new improvements or amenities you have added, tips on how to winterize your RV, favorite campfire recipes, trends in the industry, how to entertain your family in a camper when it is raining, and more. The sky is the limit.

However, this may not be something you have the time or skill to accomplish. If you or one of your team members can be the social media maven, that's great. But not every investor wants to use their time this way.

Right now, I outsource my social media to an industry-specific marketing company. When it comes to your own social media efforts, encourage your guests to post about and tag your park during their stay. One way to do this is to provide great photo opportunities, such as a large sign that identifies the location of your property, or perhaps a mascot that would make a great Instagram picture. Create photo opportunities throughout your park that encourage posting on social media.

Print Media

There was a time when everybody used print media. Parks would print out brochures and use card racks at welcome centers. Businesses and campgrounds traded their print material brochures and put ads in magazines.

In today's advertising climate, print media is going away. There are some situations where print media still works, but if you're on a budget for marketing, print is probably one of your last priorities. When talking to industry-specific marketing experts, ask them what type of print media they recommend, if any. I personally don't use any print media.

Apps

I also make sure to reach out to creators of apps that guests use to find RV parks. Some of the more popular apps include Good Sam, Allstays, The Dyrt, Campendium, and Campspot. You want to make sure they know you exist so that they can direct users to you.

Billboards and Exit Signs

Billboards and exit signs hold a different opportunity. Most people have decided where to camp before they get to you, and it is difficult to know when exactly they made that decision: Was it before they saw your sign or after? Nevertheless, billboards can still be a great source for marketing for some properties, even though their return on investment is hard to measure.

I don't personally own any properties that benefit from an exit sign or a billboard, but I have no doubt there are properties that would. For your individual property, consult with a subject-matter expert who knows RV parks and the local area. Industry-specific advertising experts can prevent you from wasting marketing dollars that may not result in returns.

Marketing for Long-Term vs. Short-Term Parks

Marketing for your long-term park will be significantly different from marketing for a short-term park. For long-term parks, I've had the best success with advertising on Craigslist and Facebook Marketplace. You simply enter the length of the site (which determines the size of the camper it can fit), the price that you're charging, whether electricity is included, and the different amenities your property offers. Include a telephone number and an email address, so the customer can get in touch with you. People who are looking to rent an RV site will not be searching in places like Apartments.com or other sites that market multifamily properties.

Chapter 17
CHECK-INS AND CHECK-OUTS

Now that you have your reservation process organized and optimized, the next stop in our journey is check-ins and check-outs. Both should have designated times to help with scheduling your workers effectively and efficiently. Guests typically check in later in the day and check out earlier, allowing you to prepare for new guests in the middle of the day.

In this chapter, we will break down the process of checking guests in and out. We will cover your options, dealing with guests who arrive late, check-in and check-out requirements, and how these processes differ between long- and short-term parks. Then we will jump into deposit methods.

Short-Term Park Check-In Process
If your park handles short-term guests, then your check-in process should be all about efficiency. In short-term parks, people will be coming and going a lot. They will expect to be able to check in at any time of the day, and many will be exhausted and ready to pull into their site when they arrive. Moreover, a fair number of reservations will come from people driving by who happened to see your campground sign late in the day and decided to pull off. You'll want to have a process that accommodates this type of late-night visitor.

That does not mean you need to staff your office all the time to allow 24/7 check-ins. Doing so is expensive and unnecessary, but you need a process in place that enables guests to check in when no one is in the office. After hours, I suggest having a mailbox station set up in front of the park or outside the office. This allows guests to check in during unstaffed hours, but you can still receive whatever information you want to gather from them.

Your guests will need parking passes, maps, receipts for their visits, and the waivers they need to sign. Any add-ons they requested when they reserved their sites, such as golf carts or permission to bring pets, require more paperwork. If your guests booked a cabin, you should also include keys to the cabin. Let's discuss each of these items briefly.

Parking Passes

Monitoring parking is for your benefit rather than the guest's. A parking pass system ensures that campers and cars are parked at their assigned sites. It also lets you know how many vehicles to expect at the site and gives you notice to redirect guests to overflow parking as needed. Passes also serve as a reminder to campers of the site numbers to look for when they arrive. This helps them confirm they are in the right spot.

Maps

The best way to help campers feel comfortable with their surroundings, find everything they need, and locate their assigned site is to give them a map. Make sure your map includes detailed information, such as the dump station, restrooms, laundry room, and any directional guidance for one-way streets. I also recommend marking their campsite on the map. Most guests do not want to search the map for their site number, especially if you have a lot of sites on your property. I'd also suggest drawing out the route to their site.

The perfect companion to a great map is good signage. Use signs like "Sites 1–20" and be generous with arrows. When people don't have good directions, they do things like turn their brights on, go down the wrong way, hit things, and park in the wrong sites. Well-drawn maps and signs help you and your guests avoid all these issues.

Receipts

Just like at any other business, it is important for you to provide guests with their proof of purchase. You do that with a receipt. This process also performs a secondary function: It gives guests a confirmation of their stay and the price they paid. It becomes far more difficult for a guest to contest the price at the conclusion of the stay when you point out they received a receipt detailing it from the beginning.

Safety Rules and Acknowledgements

I also like to include a document that lists the park's safety rules. When possible, I obtain a signature as proof that they have reviewed the rules, so they have one more reason to follow them. One easy way to do this is to have the rules listed during the online reservation process, with some sort of acknowledgement checkbox that the guest has reviewed them. At check-in, you provide a packet that includes the rules (printed out) with a statement that the guest has already acknowledged them. I find that this serves as an effective reminder both of the rules themselves and that the guest agreed to them. That packet also includes a map of the property, a parking pass, and a calendar of events happening while they are on site—assuming it applies.

I also suggest having these forms printed out in advance so that your staff doesn't need to wait for documents to print during busy check-in times. Instead, employees can simply grab the premade packets, typically with the guest's name written on it, and if any forms still need executed, the information can be filled out then.

Of course, if you go to the effort of creating an efficient process like this, you should also make guests aware of it through your website. Include information such as where to check in, what the office hours are, and where they can find their packets after hours.

I'm also a big fan of confirmation emails. These can be automated with software. Use confirmation emails to share more details as the check-in date approaches, including all the information listed above. You can also use this communication to mention favorite (or partner) local businesses and tourist destinations in the area.

Automation

Just like when you visit a McDonald's or Panera restaurant, campgrounds now have the option to use self-ordering kiosks where guests can avoid lines while checking in. Some parks even offer digital check-ins.

When check-in is fully automated, technologically savvy guests can check in without stopping at the office at all. They use their devices to review the confirmation forms and map, then drive to their site. This saves tremendous amounts of employee (and guest) time and is becoming more popular.

Some examples of fully automated solutions are Campspot, Firefly Reservations, and Newbook. They all have a self check-in option and come with software packages that help you book your park to maximum occupancy. What was once the slowest part of the entire process—checking in—can now be handled online and without staff assistance.

If you aren't using a fully automated check-in process, these services also make it easy to prepare guest packets and set them on a desk or in mailboxes for after-hours pickups. During slow periods of the day, employees can use the software to print out and prepare check-in packets. That way, when rush hour arrives, it's as simple as verifying the guest and handing them their packet. Long lines have become a thing of the past.

These platforms add new features every day, and I recommend you review the latest offerings from each when choosing which software to use. For example, some software solutions grant you the ability to create your own interactive map, which guests can use to find their site and any amenities. Many platforms automate emails and text messages, with confirmation, cancellation, and reservation information templates included. Other platforms offer the option to scan license plates, which can replace whatever parking pass system you have.

Of course, not all platform features are suitable for all parks, but software automation can significantly decrease customer wait times and the number of people coming into the office. This decreases your staffing load and will typically increase your park's ratings. Customers love efficiency. And we all hate waiting in line.

Even if you opt for an automated system, you should still provide the option for guests to physically check in at your office (assuming it isn't after hours). Some guests enjoy the personalized experience of speaking with staff and asking questions. In certain cases, it may even be necessary. If you rent out cabins or golf carts, the best way to provide keys may be to have a customer come into the office. These check-in methods need not be mutually exclusive.

Checking Out

Ideally, checking out should be just as simple as checking in. Most campers know how easy it is to check out at a hotel: You do little more than return the room key, and sometimes not even that. Campground check-outs should be just as hassle free.

One difference at an RV park may be the parking pass. Some parks require that you turn your pass in at the end of the stay, and they may provide a box to collect them on the way out. However, with the above-mentioned license plate scanning system, even that process is eliminated. The more that you can make the check-out process as simple as driving out, the easier it will be on you and your staff.

Assigning Tasks before Check-Out

Some campgrounds have a check-out process that is similar to a vacation rental or Airbnb. In these scenarios, a guest might be required to complete a few minor tasks before driving off. For example, you may ask that they clean up any trash left at their site and bring it to a central location. Whatever you ask them to do, make it easy. Guests should not have to wait in line to check out, and you don't want their last memory to be that of frustration.

Long-Term Parks

Unlike short-term parks, long-term parks typically require more extensive check-ins and check-outs. Long-term parks function more like residences than hotels, and residents will need to take care of the property to avoid bringing in bugs and wild critters that could cause damage at your park. At check-in, you will want to go over rules such as what guests can have outside their RVs and how they are expected to maintain their sites. You will also place more responsibilities on the RV park guests since you won't have staff going around to every site to clean up trash.

Limiting What Residents Can Leave Outside

In long-term parks, the most important rules involve what residents can leave outside their RV or cabin. You might think this is intuitive or that RV dwellers won't have large items to set outside. But in my experience, it's shocking what some people will bring.

I've seen everything from full-sized grills to patio furniture. Tarps, gas cans, and even outdoor refrigerators have made appearances. I have even seen people unpack garden gnomes to set their spot apart from others. The bottom line is to limit what people can leave out. For example, tarps collect mosquitoes, so those should be off-limits, no matter what the justification might be. Refrigerators are in a similar category, as they are not only a target for animals, but they can also be a suffocation hazard for children. I recommend you do your research on whether outdoor refrigerators are allowed in your park's city or state. If you want to allow refrigerators (and I admittedly own one park in which I allow them), make sure there are strict rules on where they are placed.

Also, review your rules on whether food can be stored in a car or RV. In some locations, the risk of bears and raccoons finding the food is so great that parks put a ban on food storage in vehicles. For these types of parks, you may consider building bear boxes that can be rented out for profit. That way, you are not only offering a service, but you are also increasing your revenue stream.

Gas cans are yet another hazard. I strongly encourage making a rule that gas cans should never be left sitting under an RV. This is a fire hazard and a threat to anyone in the RV.

You might also consider setting a limit for the number of things people can have outside. At my combination parks, I tend to permit one patio set, one grill, and a few personal items. Allowing more than a few could lead to someone setting up a bunch of garden gnomes around their site. You don't want that, nor do you want people setting up multiple grills and patio sets when one of each is all that is necessary.

However, if your park is only for long-term camping, you can be a little more lenient. In these scenarios, your guidelines might include how and where guests should store extra items. Fences may also be permitted at long-term parks. These can be justifiable when there are dogs that reside with their owners.

In general, the most important thing you can do in any of these scenarios is to be specific. Have standards that guests are well aware of, and make sure you have their signatures of acknowledgement.

Keeping Things Clean

Another big difference between short-term parks and long-term parks is who carries the burden to keep the place clean. With long-term parks, that's on the guests.

I like to hold people to some level of order and cleanliness by having an annual cleaning day. Each year, my teams send out flyers calling for a spring cleaning to the guests. On a specified date, we order a dumpster for people to discard things they don't need. As extra encouragement, we host a large cookout and/or order pizzas. Keeping your park clean should be a high priority because a more pristine park is more appealing to guests.

Wrapping It Up

Checking guests in can be a slow, demanding process, but it must be done. Everyone who comes to your park must complete all the check-in requirements, and that includes filling out forms and potentially picking up a couple of items before arriving at the site.

These various steps might seem like a lot to manage, especially when customers arrive late and the office is closed. For this reason, I highly recommend you consider operating your park using reservation software and opt for solutions that provide online check-in and check-out. Investigate how the software's additional features can streamline other processes (like parking and maps) as well.

Now that your guests are checked in and ready to enjoy their stay, let's dig into what you can do daily to manage your park with efficiency.

Chapter 13
MANAGING THE DAY-TO-DAY ROUTINES

Keeping up with business at an RV park is not easy. It gets harder as you expand your park and offer more customizations and add-ons for guests. Although some difficulties never go away, they will get easier as you gain more experience and learn more about the ins and outs of your park.

This is especially true if you follow certain routines and maintain guidelines for guests and employees. We've already gone over some procedures, such as dealing with large groups and finding the best employees, but let's explore more specifics and review how you can maintain a clean park and manage a multitude of accommodations.

In day-to-day operations, my first rule is to have explicit processes in place. For example, have a well-documented system. Make sure your staff knows what your parking, long-term stay, and pet policies are. If a customer shows up with questions about your policies, your staff should know them like the back of their hands and have printouts ready to refer to as needed.

My second rule is to make your day-to-day operations so efficient and a routine that customers look on in admiration. Site checks? Make them like clockwork. Trash and nuisances? The staff should identify issues before guests even notice them.

Customer satisfaction is critical. Hands down, it is the most important part of maintaining an RV park. Without satisfied customers, you lose your base of income and, eventually, the entire business. I'm going to spend this chapter discussing how your day-to-day operations can set your park up for ideal customer satisfaction.

TIP: Customer satisfaction is critical

Site Checks

Daily site checks are a critical aspect of daily management and can set your park up for success, if done correctly. If you don't know what is going on in your park, you can't address issues before they become emergencies, and you won't know about problems before the customers do. The last thing you want is to have a park where you are always reacting to customer complaints. If a problem has risen to a level where the customers notice, you aren't satisfying them. Site checks give you an eagle-eyed view of everything you need to know.

When you or your staff members conduct site checks, walk—don't drive—through your park, and make sure every site is as it should be. When you walk, you see more. You see little pieces of paper blowing around. You notice cars that don't have parking passes. You see the trash bin that is surprisingly full or a water spigot that a guest left turned partially on. These are things that well-trained staff can look out for and address before the customer has even noticed.

Site checks also ensure that other staff members have completed their jobs and did not miss anything. Many times, if cleaners feel rushed, they miss things. A site check provides a second set of eyes to make sure the next guest will find the place perfectly welcoming.

Management can also use this time to check on public areas at the park and to confirm that the maintenance crew members have finished their tasks, such as raking leaves, trimming, weeding, and repairing any malfunctioning utilities.

In my parks, my management teams complete site checks twice a day. And just to make sure these checks are top of mind and automated, I have my managers set reminder alarms.

There's also some strategy in timing the site checks. In my case, I have staff complete site checks at RV sites at 11:00 a.m. and at alternative accommodations at 2:30 p.m. At my parks, RVs check out at 11:00, and the next guests can check in as early as noon. By walking the RV sites at 11:00 (not noon or 1:00 p.m.), my staff can double-check that all campers who are checking out that day have either left or are nearly done packing up. If we see guests who don't even appear to be packing up on their last day, we can talk with them to confirm their intentions.

You might think that conducting these site checks can seem domineering or that customers might feel put off by them. I've found exactly the opposite to be true. During this high-activity time, customers see that you care immensely about your park. They see you addressing every small detail. This visible attention to detail has dramatically improved my customer service. Since implementing these automated site checks, my positive reviews have increased tremendously, and my negative reviews have dropped. Some customers see these site checks and attention to detail as their last memory of the park, which isn't a bad thing.

Managers should be aware of both park conditions and staff tasks. You may even want to create a list to remind your managers and staff what the chores are. This level of organization shows that you care about completion of chores, and there's a clear expectation of who is doing what.

Extra People

Here's another piece of information that site checks give you: knowledge of when more people than anticipated are staying at a site. At my parks, we assign a recommended maximum number of people at each site. When you do site checks, you can confirm that maximum and take note of whether the site will need more frequent attention due to the size or activities of the group. Since more guests inevitably leads to increased use of public facilities, I have my managers check on large groups a little more often. This also tends to keep them from getting out of control and impacting other campers.

With extra people, there will be other things you need to approach differently. For one, you may want the pricing to differ based on how many people travel in one camper. For example, some parks set the standard price for two people and charge extra (maybe $5 or $10) for each additional person. Other parks set the base price at groups of four. How you set your fees will depend on what your park has to offer.

I use a family-centered approach at my parks, especially since many of my resorts are near tourist destinations. I price per family, using a base price for two adults and two children. You may also want to set standard pricing for other accommodation options, such as cabins. If you have cabins on your property, you can generate a price based on how many people can comfortably stay in them. I have cabins that sleep eight, so I charge cabin rentals as if they are for eight people and charge extra for any additional people.

These extra charges are ways for you to make up for the money that goes into electricity, Wi-Fi, water, and other utility bills. Plus, you'll likely need to purchase more toilet paper for the restrooms and increase the number of chemicals in your pool to compensate for people taking up more space in it. Generally, the more people on site, the more everything is used, the higher the cost, and the greater the need for consistent cleaning and site checks. As you become more familiar with your park and the types of groups that visit, you will be able to better gauge how to price everything.

Long-Term Parks

Long-term RV parks necessitate a different approach to most of these considerations. At a long-term park, guests should be treated as they would at a mobile home park or an apartment complex. The lease should list all the long-term inhabitants for that site, and guests staying for more than a couple of days should be identified pursuant to a policy.

There are a couple of reasons for this. First, you want background checks on everyone living on your property. You don't have that luxury with extra guests, so their stays should be temporary. Second, extra guests means extra utility consumption. Although most of the cost will go to the owner of the RV, the burden of some utilities (such as the water bill) may fall on you.

I'm stopping short of saying your residents can't have guests or visitors; I believe that's overly restrictive. Rather, I believe in monitoring the extent of an extra guest's stay. Set a rule for how long a guest is allowed to visit before they are considered a resident. Include these guidelines in your tenant agreement documents, and check your local regulations regarding tenancy. Some states and cities already have rules in place for how long guests of residents can occupy rental properties or mobile home parks. I would follow those standards for your long-term parks to be on the safe side. For example, in California a guest can stay with a resident for twenty consecutive days or thirty separate days in a year, and they will not have to pay. Most states follow a similar pattern, limiting stays based on consecutive and nonconsecutive days. When your tenants allow guests to stay past that mark, they must register the extra occupants and pay for their stay.

Parking and Charges for Vehicles

Parking at an RV park and campground can easily become chaotic, particularly when your property is near a tourist area. In these cases, encourage guests to bring a single vehicle, because you simply won't have the room for every guest to bring two. This "encouragement" can be done via parking fees.

If you don't monitor the number of vehicles, it's easy to end up with cars in the streets or blocked traffic. This issue is amplified when your park is close to a tourist destination. Visitors will sometimes welcome friends and family to your RV park or travel together to the tourist destination via RV. They treat your park as a parking lot, and your campground starts to resemble event parking more than an inviting retreat.

If you are feeling unjustified in imposing parking restrictions and fees, remember this: You paid hundreds of thousands of dollars per acre to get a location that was desirable. Your guests agree that it's a desirable place, or they wouldn't invite others to park. It is completely justifiable to charge for this service you are offering and to increase the charges as needed until you aren't looking at a sea of vehicles in your campground.

Also, charging parking fees is a common practice. Don't feel like you are a Scrooge for wanting to keep your park in order. At one of my properties, we charge $10 per added vehicle to afford a bonus parking area.

You may also consider a towing policy (post a sign for this) for vehicles that park without parking passes. You only have a limited number of spaces, and violators can cost you money as well as customer satisfaction. Although it isn't necessary, you may also want to number your spaces so that you don't have large vehicles or trucks taking up two parking spaces when they only paid for one.

Even at your long-term parks, you will need to prepare for parking issues. People tend to have more vehicles than they need. Often, they have an RV and two cars to drive around town. Add in their visitors, broken-down or stored vehicles, and rental cars, and you have yourself another parking lot. In your rules and guidelines, list your parking expectations very clearly. I tend to allow two cars per site and charge for any usage that starts to impact the livability of the park. Inevitably, people still break the limit, and we have to remind them that they're not allowed to have more than two vehicles. However, if you don't stay on top of this issue, your property will look sloppy, which will ultimately bring down its value and the amount people are willing to pay per month.

Long-Term Leases and Legal Considerations

If you own a long-term park, I highly encourage you to find an attorney in the RV park industry and have them draw up your lease agreement. By using an industry expert, you ensure that all your guidelines are compliant with state guidelines, and you aren't permitting illegal behavior. Additionally, when you use a legal expert, your up-front cost will be more than recouped within the first year, and you will minimize the chance that one tenant can ruin your entire investment.

This also gives you the opportunity to ask questions about your area's laws, regulations, and general best practices. Statutes are not always a Google search away, so attorneys can provide guidance on how to host long-term residents on your property. Apart from their legal expertise, having a lawyer draft the agreement also protects your rights as a landlord. Let's look at how and why a well-written lease can help you.

State in your lease agreement that you, the landowner, are not responsible for anything that happens to a resident's RV. If you don't include that clause, you will end up paying more than you should. Let me provide an example. On more than one occasion, I've had guests plug their older campers into my new power boxes, and something would go wrong. This inevitably leads to complaints like, "Your power box caused my problems. I need you to replace this, and this, and this."

In each case, I had electricians come out and confirm that there was nothing wrong with our equipment; the problem was their old camper. If you have a clause in your contract, you can point to it to show guests that they are responsible for their own property, regardless of what happens. And frankly, that's the way it should be. Park owners can't be responsible for every type of vehicle that pulls into the park.

> **TIP: Make sure that you, the landowner, are not responsible for anything that happens to a resident's rv.**

Another necessity on your lease are site guidelines. As I advised earlier, include all of the rules tenants must follow regarding what they can and cannot have on their property. Check with your state and city campground rules to ensure all gaps are covered. Your list of rules should include how many objects people can have outside their campers, what items are allowed to sit outside, how many cars they are allowed to have at their site, your limitations on pets, expectations of outdoor cleanliness, and any other guidelines you feel are necessary.

You are likely familiar with the rest of the key elements in a lease if you have ever rented anything before. The agreement should include the rental cost, the payment frequency, how payment is made, what payment covers, etc. While your attorney can help you with all these clauses, it's best if you write down your general terms in advance so that your lease agreement includes everything you want. Keep an original copy of the agreement and provide a copy to your tenant. This is your—and their—reference sheet and proof that they promised to comply with your park standards.

Long-Term Pets

Although you can prohibit pets entirely, you may lose out on more potential customers by doing so. Most RV owners seem to have pets, and it is unlikely that they will give them up to stay at your park; they will find another park that allows pets. Hence, you'll probably want to allow pets on your property.

Pet rules should also be included in your lease agreement. These rules need to be very specific so that you can easily refer to them if you and your guests have any issues. But before you start setting pet guidelines, make sure you first talk with your insurance company. Some insurers will already have a few barriers in place. For example, some companies list which breeds of pets are not allowed on your property, whereas other companies are not as picky. By knowing your insurance company's pet policies, you can build your rules around theirs.

For example, if you want to restrict the ownership of large dogs, don't use the term "large dogs." Choose a weight amount and add a clause such as "dogs over 35 pounds." This degree of specificity lets you easily confirm if a guest has violated the rules. Another method is to restrict the number of pets per camper. I highly recommend applying this second option, even though both are good. You would be surprised at how many pets people squeeze into one trailer. I typically set my cap amount to two pets. Two is a reasonable number and manageable for everyone. I also comply with my insurance and bar a few breeds, such as German shepherds, pit bulls, Doberman pinschers, wolf mixes, and rottweilers.

Other pet guidelines consist of the nitty-gritty policies. You will want people to clean up after their pets and keep them on leashes (that includes cats) when they are outside. To encourage your guest to follow these standards, you could provide stations for the pets with poop bags and disposal areas or a small fenced-in dog park to let their dogs off leash outside. Another rule to consider is not allowing pets to be left unsupervised outside, even if they are on a leash. A pet that manages to get loose can cause distress throughout the camp. Pets left outside could also attract attacks from other animals, particularly at night.

The rest of the guidelines are up to you. But the most important point is to make sure your rules are specific, so there are no misunderstandings when it comes to enforcement.

Handling Money

Day-to-day operations include yet another important topic: how you manage money at your park. The last thing you want is a theft or break-in because someone knows you keep money on hand, which is why I highly recommend making daily deposits to your bank account.

When I first started in the business, most payments were made with cash. By the end of the day, we had substantial amounts of it in the cash drawers, which was always a worry to me. These days, most reservations are made in advance via credit card. Only 10 percent or so are paid for in cash. Even with paid reservations, you will inevitably have some cash in the office.

If you happen to be at a smaller park, you may think $100 or so at the end of the day doesn't merit the trip. If this is the case, I suggest having a minimum threshold rule. For example, if you hit $500 in cash, you make a deposit. And enforce it strictly. Staff members can get used to a relaxed schedule during the offseason where they go to the bank once or twice a week. Don't let this carry over to the busy season, or you could find yourself the victim of a theft of tens of thousands of dollars.

Chapter 19

OPERATING SITES AND SURROUNDINGS

RV parks can have several physical aspects that distinguish themselves from each other. This chapter details some of the best amenities and upgrades to add to your park. Additionally, as we discuss in this book, these amenities and upgrades can give your park significant additional sources of revenue.

Upgraded Roads

Before you plan too many upgrades, you should first determine where your roads and pathways will be and what kind of pavement you will use. You can use gravel, sand, asphalt, concrete, or other options for site surfaces. You do not need to pave every road and site. However, your ratings will improve if you pave your streets.

I recommend choosing one or two forms of pavement and using the same theme throughout the park. In other words, if you choose concrete for a road and gravel for a site, use concrete for every road and gravel for every site. Of course, you should always check local regulations to confirm your compliance.

At one of my parks, I use gravel roadways, and some parts of every site are concrete. Guests have been pleased with that mix. Even though gravel is not always the preferred ground material, it is fairly easy to maintain and a cost-effective option. At other parks, I have used gravel throughout. If you do it properly, a full-gravel park can still look sharp.

The most expensive option is to pave your entire park. That can approach hundreds of thousands of dollars, especially for the larger parks. Gravel is less expensive, but keep in mind that the expenses are recurring; you will need to add more gravel every few years. Therefore, you need to consider gravel one of your routine capital expenses. Your park will start to look neglected if you skimp on gravel maintenance.

Gates

Once you have finalized your roads and paths, you can consider permanent fixtures like security gates. More and more parks are adding gates at their entrances, and for good reason. When you install gates, you provide both physical and psychological benefits to your guests.

Physical and Psychological Safety

First and foremost, gates serve as an additional measure of safety. They require guests to either have a code or call-in to enter, which prevents people from just wandering in to look around.

The psychological benefit is also significant. Gates offer guests an immediate sense of physical security. For most of your visitors, your park is a far-off, unknown destination. You could be located just two miles from a well-traveled tourist attraction, but that won't stop people from worrying about the dark corners of your property and the bad actors who might find their way into the park.

When you install a security gate, you send a clear message: We only want people who belong here. Does a sign that says "Registered Guests Only" communicate the same message? Technically, yes, but it's never perceived the same way. Gates make it clear that your efforts to protect those on the inside from perceived threats on the outside are sincere. If you are willing to install a gate, you are willing to go to greater lengths to safeguard your guests. People will associate cameras, night guards, roaming rottweilers, and other security measures with your park, whether or not you actually use them.

When your guests stroll around your park, you want them to feel as safe as they might feel at home. Your park should be inviting and restful. Their mind should not be on what lurks behind the corner. If it is, it's doubtful they will ever associate your park with a peaceful vacation.

Another psychological impact of gates is the feeling of privacy or separation from the community outside the park. Some might say gates portray exclusivity. In my mind, there's nothing wrong with that portrayal. Your park should feel exclusive. The more you can make it feel like a resort, the more you attract guests, and the more you can charge. It's even better if your park has its own attractions or amenities. One of my parks is in a popular rafting and cycling area, and the built-in attractions of the park draw a large crowd. By staying at my park, guests have access to these beautiful, natural amenities that they wouldn't have had otherwise.

Now imagine if my guests realized that anyone could drive in and use the same amenities. Their access is no longer exciting and exclusive. They might even start thinking, *Hey, why did I pay extra for what others get for free?*

Financial Benefit

By limiting access to your park, you also benefit. Your utility bills are lower because you don't have as many patrons. You don't have to clean the public areas as much, because the traffic is reduced. And there's something else about human nature that I've found: When people pay to have access, they take better care of their surroundings. Give something to people for free, and they suddenly devalue it. They throw trash on the ground. They don't clean up after themselves. This is yet another psychological as well as financial benefit of gated access and the aura of exclusivity. People care more about keeping it that way.

Choosing a Gate

Gates come in multiple forms, and you should choose what is best for your park. You might choose to use a gate with key cards or a keypad with codes, weight-sensitive gates, or even a guard posted at the gate. Each method has its benefits and drawbacks.

Key cards

Key cards are an option for short-term parks in that guests need not memorize a code; they just use the cards and return them at checkout. Cards can be issued with check-in packets, and you typically ask for guests to drop them in a box as they leave. Key cards provide the advantage of giving you complete control over their use. You can turn them on and off instantly through your computer, eliminating any worry that a lost key card will lead to a new, unpaid, long-term resident at your park.

The biggest detriment, however, is the cost associated with the cards. Guests often forget to return them or lose them. For this reason, you may want to charge a refundable $5 fee up front for the key card, providing an incentive for its return. Although key cards are not my favorite choice, I want to share this as a potential option.

Keypads

For long-term parks, I tend to prefer keypads. In this case, a resident can have long-term access using the same code for weeks or months at a time. Because guests are long term rather than short term, it is not as imperative to change the codes regularly. The pool of those with code knowledge is relatively small compared to short-term parks, where there is daily turnover. I share the code with guests through a confirmation email or upon check-in.

With the latest keypads, it is also possible to assign each user a code. While this is a little more difficult to administer and track than a global-use code, user-based codes allow you to know when each resident comes in and out, and you can better monitor if they are giving out the code to unauthorized guests.

Weight-Sensitive Gates

Another option is installing a gate that senses the weight of an automobile and then opens. This can provide a deterrent, since would-be thieves may think you are monitoring them in some way. And it provides some sense of security for the residents. But overall, the protections in this system are minimal. Anyone with a vehicle can still come and go without a card or code.

Guarded Gates

The ultimate level of security and exclusivity can be obtained with guarded gates, where guards monitor and document everyone who enters and leaves the park. However, this is also the costliest of options. You will need to hire several security guards to take shifts at the entrance, and you will need to build and provide utilities to a guardhouse. At the same time, though, your property value will increase, and you can demand a higher price from guests. This option can be financially feasible if you are in a location where its security and exclusivity will be valued.

Of course, all of the above gate options mean extra expenses. Any automatic gate will increase your electricity bill. Add a guard to that, and your monthly fees increase significantly. As you consider whether the cost is outweighed by the increase in value, consider if your guests are short term or long term, what crowds your location attracts, and the level of security you think is most appropriate for your location.

Signage

Create a budget for installing and updating signs for your park. Just like any other signs you see when driving on the interstate, park signs help first-time visitors know where they are going.

You may think that providing digital or paper maps at check-in is sufficient, but you'd be wrong. People can quickly become lost without good signage, and lost visitors driving large vehicles can lead to disastrous situations. Put simply, signs pay for themselves in the long run. Use them generously.

Entrance Signs

The first sign to consider is your entrance sign. At a minimum, it should have the park's name, and it should be lit. Make sure it has high visibility from the road, and clear away trees, bushes, or grass that may block the visibility from a distance or certain angles.

If you haven't purchased a commercial sign before, allow me to prepare you: The cost will be shocking. My first experience with this was certainly a memorable one. More than a decade ago, I sought a quote for my first (single) sign. It was $30,000. I thought they were out of their minds, and I considered going forward without a sign.

But that would have been a mistake. As it turns out, I received so many more reservations over the next few months simply because I had a sign. I often asked people how they heard about our park, and I was pleasantly surprised by how many said, "We saw your sign!"

I estimate that I earned back the entirety of my $30,000 investment within the first year of opening my park. Let that serve as guidance for you as you try to justify the initial expense. (You'll likely pay more than $30,000, as my quote was from ten years ago.) Your entrance sign not only lets people know that your park exists, but it is also the first impression most people will have of your park. With that in mind, I recommend you put some thought into the design. You want people to notice it, remember it, and like it.

Park Signs

Next, you need to plan out the signs inside your park. One must-have is a sign for your office. People need to know where they can go to check in and get information. It's also the first place they will go and their first exposure to your staff. Don't make it a confusing experience.

You also want to specify street names and directions, using signs to point guests to the different parts of the property. Also, if you have a loop that goes around the site and you've set it up to be unidirectional (one way only), make sure you use signs to clarify which way is correct. This unidirectional format works well in an RV park because many sites are set at an angle, and there's no way to get in if you come from the opposite direction. But what happens if you don't have signs that clearly indicate the direction of travel? Accidents. Angry guests. Attempts to enter the site from ridiculous angles. I've seen them all, and I don't recommend you go there.

Another critical set of signs are those that identify the sites. Picture your guests arriving on a rainy evening, peering through their windows to see the site numbers before they back into their spots. If the signs don't clearly point out which site is theirs, with fonts that are easily read from a distance, you'll have people camping in the wrong spots—something we've already discussed as time consuming, reservation disrupting, and frustrating to everyone.

You'll also need signs for cabins, glamping locations, and the nearest facilities. You will want signs on the road that label which site numbers are found in each cul-de-sac or side road, such as a sign that directs campers to "Sites 1–20" with an arrow pointing to the right and another sign with an upward arrow toward the rest of the sites. The next side street may have a sign for "Sites 21–40," etc.

Signage is helpful when office staff members give directions to visitors. They can reference the signs and streets to let them know where to go. For instance, when people check in for a cabin stay, staff members may direct them to "drive around the curve until you see a sign that illustrates a cabin with an arrow pointing up. Drive up the hill in the direction of that arrow, and just past the bathrooms, you will find the cabins." That will make your guests aware of what signs they need to look for: one with a cabin and one for bathrooms.

When making all your signs, you should follow some general standards. First, your posts must be easy to read and understand. If you use clip art for a sign, it needs to be an easily recognizable object that directly represents what it is supposed to. For the sake of comprehension, I would stick to words for most (if not all) of your park signs. At the very least, include the word with the image. Use arrows on signs to point people in the right direction, but be sure that they make sense to others.

Also, use reasonable colors for signs. You want the words or images on them to be visible at night. White letters on a medium-to-dark background are probably the best route to go. If you do not have good lighting near your signs, they need to be reflective, so drivers can still see them. Use road signage as an example to follow.

Hookups

The term "hookups" refers to your utilities: sewer, power, water, and sometimes cable TV. In general, campers expect a power pedestal and water. Power pedestals need to have 30- and 50-amp options. That also means that your box must be 110 volts, because 30-amp RV plugs can only run on 110, while 50-amps work with either 110 or 220 volts.

These utility posts typically also supply water and cable. The type of pedestals you have will depend on the location of your park. If you are in states like Louisiana and Florida, where flooding is common, you will want marine-grade pedestals because they are designed to work despite routine floods. For zones without much flood risk, less-expensive options will suffice.

In general, you should set the goal of developing or converting every RV site in your park into a full-hookup site. That means providing the power and water pedestal, as well as a sewer hookup. These sites are desirable for more experienced campers, and guests will be willing to pay more for them.

Note that not all RVs have sewer outputs in the same place. Some are in the middle of the RV; some are in the rear. Because of this, you may consider providing two sewer hookup locations for every site, especially if you are doing a fresh build or redesign. By doing so, you allow guests to maximize their camping space without having to worry about long hoses winding around their RV.

In a less-preferable situation, where the park doesn't provide sewer hookups at the site, the park may offer a dump station in a central location where campers can dispose of their waste after their stay. A fee can also be assessed for this service. However, keep in mind that this is not the preferred method for seasoned RV campers. It requires the guest to hold their sewage while camping in their site, which sometimes overflows inside the RV. In other situations, the smell of the holding tanks can become rank. There are all types of products designed to combat this odor, but the bottom line is this type of site is less desirable. Full site hookups are so strongly preferred that some people pass by campgrounds that don't offer them.

Remember that before anyone hooks up all their power cords, water hoses, and tanks, the breaker pedestal must be off. This prevents dangerous electrical issues and damaging the hookups. Once they are all hooked up, then the guest can turn the breaker on. Guests should turn off the breaker again before disconnecting. Because this is a safety issue, I recommend putting a warning sign on the breaker pedestal directing users to turn it off during plugging and unplugging.

Since you are not a national park, where minimal amenities are the norm, your guests expect a pedestal at their site. If your sites aren't up to modern standards, I'd certainly put pedestals and sewer hookups in your long-term budget.

Site Cleanup

You may be thinking that, unlike cabins, RV sites will rarely need your attention. Unfortunately, there are campers who will defy this logic, and you'd be surprised how much of a mess they can leave behind. Since no one wants to pull into a site that looks like a dump, let's discuss how to prepare sites between guests.

If you have a mix of rocks or dirt with concrete, the previous visitors may have tracked some debris onto the site. Simply using a broom can resolve many of these issues. However, some people chew gum and spit it out on the concrete. Others leave trash behind. Firepits may be full of debris, and sometimes winds bring in leaves, sticks, and grass clippings. Employees should also look at the picnic table to make sure it is positioned out of the way and not blocking anyone from pulling in. Uniform sites will give guests the feeling that they can expect the same type of perfection every time.

To accomplish everything needed in one visit, I have my maintenance team bring more than just their brooms, just in case. A shovel and bucket can be useful for cleaning dirty firepits.

Your outdoor sites will generally require a small investment of your time: repositioning a table and picking up a few pieces of trash. But be prepared for the occasional disaster, because customers expect a tidy site. It's where they will spend most of their time, so make sure they feel at home.

Work Orders

Work orders will be your new best friend. If you have a complaint, there's a work order. If a manager notices something needs to be fixed, there's a work order. Anytime there's a request for anything, whether it's related to the grounds, housekeeping, or maintenance, and it's not something that needs to be tended to immediately, you'll write a work order.

These work orders are the list of what you divvy up to your staff each day. For example, maybe one of the doorknobs is broken in the bathhouse, and your maintenance team has gone home for the day. Since you likely have numerous bathrooms, a single broken doorknob is not a critical issue. It can wait for your maintenance staff to return in the morning.

This is how you make the list of work orders (called a "work list") function for you. Each morning, take everything that was turned in the previous day and assign it to the respective teams. Put the critical or emergency items at the top, then add those that are not as critical or time sensitive lower on the list. In this case, the work list for maintenance will include fixing the broken doorknob.

Work lists can be created using pen and paper, or you can use an app. For those owners who prefer to automate everything, it is common to use software or apps to collect work orders and assign them electronically.

I'll throw in a word of caution here: Consider your audience. My best maintenance guy can't read, and many of my work campers share their phones with their spouses. Some don't have smartphones at all, and some rural campsites don't have great Wi-Fi or cellular reception. If you use a high-tech system with an app for these workers or locations, you haven't gained any improvement in efficiency. Depending on your staff and location, the old-school method of pen and paper can sometimes be the best way to make a work list.

On-site Manager

Many RV parks have options for workers to live on-site. In these cases, you could put your manager as close as possible to guests. And as you look at RV parks, you will see many different options to create convenient living quarters for staff. Sometimes you'll see the owner or managers living in a camper, so you can use an RV site for that. Sometimes there is a great stick-built house on-site, and the manager lives there. There's sometimes an apartment inside your check-in office where that manager or owner lives. It really doesn't matter what accommodations that you have for them; it's just important that somebody is close by or on-site to take care of anything that might go wrong.

Groundskeeping

Groundskeeping (mowing, weeding, and landscaping) is one of the things on your property that you'll have to decide whether to contract out or keep in house. For the first nine years of my park ownership, we managed our grounds internally. I had extra staff to keep up with the mowing, weeding, and all the various yard work. Two years ago, I switched to having a landscaping company come in and do it once a week, and it is much more efficient to have the landscaping company do these tasks.

When you are choosing which is better for your property, I recommend figuring out how many labor hours it takes to do it yourself and the cost of powering and maintaining the equipment, and then get a quote from a couple of landscaping companies to decide which option to choose.

Landscaping

Landscape design is another significant factor that impacts both the beauty and value of your property. Landscapers may help with things such as mowing, weeding, flowerpots, etc. When you landscape, you want to do something simple but attractive. You don't want significant upkeep, because you pay for that. You also want to consider the cost of watering plants. Here are my recommendations when it comes to the various aspects of landscaping.

Trees

RV parks tend to have a love-hate relationship with trees. Guests want to camp among them, but they don't want them to damage their campers as they pull in and out. Also, guests want their cable, internet, and satellite systems to work. The more trees you have, the less likely those things are to work. What I strive for is a good mix between mature trees and some clearance so that people's devices still work.

Have your trees maintained regularly. Using a licensed service to cut limbs and dying trees is something you need to budget for annually. One dying tree could ruin someone's life and your business. Unfortunately, our industry is filled with stories of trees and limbs falling on campers and tents. Make it a priority to minimize the chances of that happening at your property.

Posts

Posts can serve another important role: to protect the equipment behind them. We are seeing record numbers of first-time campers, and there is a learning curve to driving an RV or trailer. And even the most experienced drivers sometimes miss something. Blind spots exist, and sometimes the darkness of night prevents drivers from seeing hazards. By putting posts as a barrier to equipment, you are both protecting the equipment and making it more visible. You're also protecting your investment.

Posts aren't the only option. You can have a fence or boulders—the sky's the limit on what landscaping elements you could use. The main goal is to protect your equipment without cheapening the look of your park.

Lighting

Lighting is another critical purchase for your park. It needs to accomplish two competing purposes: be bright enough to help guests see hazards but not so bright that it interrupts sleep. Most lighting decisions are personal preference, but you want to be conscious of impacting the guests. You do not want your park to resemble a big-box store parking lot that glows at night. Find a lighting solution that provides enough light for people to see obstacles while driving or walking, but not so much that you get complaints from campers who are unable to sleep.

Trash

Before I bought my first park, I traveled across the country in a camper, staying at every type of property I could find. Ten years later, I did the same thing with my kids in tow. Those cross-country trips gave me a wide view of the varying types of properties that exist in many regions of the country.

These trips also provided me with the critical perspective of what it is like to be a guest. One of the things that drove me the craziest on both trips, ten years apart, was having to take my trash to the dumpster.

Before you jump to the conclusion that I'm some snooty brat who doesn't really like camping, let me set the record straight. In my case, and I believe I'm not alone, my RV was already packed. Asking me to drag the trash across the park, while I'm single parenting three kids, is more of a chore than it needs to be. Not only that, but it also zaps the feeling of being on vacation when I have to haul around my trash.

An alternative option—and there are parks that do this—is to have maintenance drive through the park once a day and pick up bagged garbage. In those parks, campers can leave their trash in front of their campers at a specific time each morning.

I'm not a fan of this option either. First, if you happen to be strolling through the park at garbage pickup time, the park looks and smells horrible. Moreover, it's an invitation to animals. Have you seen what a raccoon can do to garbage?

Based on my cross-country trips, I chose to implement a different option at my parks: I've added trash bins at every other site. Maintenance still comes by and picks up garbage a time or two every day, but I've eliminated all the other issues I mentioned above.

Winterization

If you're in a park that gets below 40°F and you have alternative accommodations, such as rental campers, you must winterize them before freezing temperatures burst the pipes in your unit. Burst pipes cost a lot of money, do a lot of damage, and in some cases destroy the camper. To prevent this, I set a certain date by which all eligible accommodations are to be winterized. Then I make sure it's on my calendar with an alert.

Not sure how to winterize? YouTube is a great instructor on this topic. Look for the type of campers you have, and you'll undoubtedly find some great step-by-step tutorials.

Also, make sure you remember to un-winterize them come spring.

Smoking

I ban smoking in all my parks. You don't want somebody smoking in your alternative accommodation, because you will never get that smell out, and your next guest will (rightfully) complain and write terrible reviews that you will have a difficult time recovering from.

If you also choose to prohibit smoking, set a smoking policy on your website, signage, and a waiver that guests sign. I also include signage inside the accommodations that ban smoking and charge a $200 fee for violations. You also don't want guests smoking at your amenities, like the pool, playground, or bathhouse. To that end, make sure you have signage throughout your property and a designated smoking area, if you choose to have one.

Make sure your employees understand that these restrictions apply to them as well. It's not a good look to have your employees riding around on a golf cart smoking or standing outside the office front door lighting up a cigarette when the campers are forbidden from doing so. To make things simple, my policy is that employees cannot smoke while in uniform. I do provide, however, a designated smoking area behind the office where employees can't be seen by any guests. Here, they can have their scheduled breaks and a cigarette if they're smokers.

Phones

Depending on what city you're in, you may be required to add an emergency phone outside of your pool area. Make sure that this phone only calls 911. You also want to make sure that the phone is clearly labeled as strictly an emergency phone.

We used to have a phone at one of my parks that would call other numbers, and as you might imagine, people would just sit up there using it for who knows what. You can find a call-limited emergency phone on Amazon, which is what I use at my parks.

Fire Extinguishers

Most cities require that you have fire extinguishers, and these aren't the regular fire extinguishers that you might find at Walmart or Lowe's. They need to be inspected and certified annually by the fire marshal. This is a requirement not only for the office and other buildings, but also for each alternative accommodation. Your local fire department will be the most reliable resource for the details on these requirements.

Brochure Stand

If you're in an area that has any kind of attractions, people will constantly come into your office asking if they can put out some information about what they're offering. On the one hand, your guests want to know what's going on in the area, and it's important for you to provide resources in that regard. On the other hand, a kiosk clutters up your office and takes up space that could otherwise be used for items you sell. That's money lost.

Because I have parks in tourist towns, I know that my guests would benefit from a brochure stand, but I also don't want to take up the space in my office. The way I satisfy both needs is I position the stands near the laundry room, so when guests come into the office and ask what's going on locally, we can direct them to this area.

Most people do an internet search or have their excursions planned ahead of time, but brochures are still something that guests often ask about. Brochures aren't limited to area attractions; people who do things like camper washing, maintenance, or repairs will want to advertise. When those people come into your office, I highly recommend that you say, "The only way that your brochures can be on property or that I can recommend you is if I have a copy of your insurance." Otherwise, if something goes wrong, you may end up liable because you've recommended them to your guests. I also find that this reduces the number of people who leave their materials.

Cameras

A couple years ago, we had a problem where showerheads kept going missing. These weren't fancy; they were $20 Lowe's showerheads. I have no idea why people kept stealing them, but they did.

I already knew I needed to add cameras to the property anyway, but that was my extra push to put in a camera system. We added cameras all over the property. They were installed in the office, at the bathhouses (outside, not inside), in the laundry room, at the pools, and near the glamping tents.

Cameras are now positioned throughout my properties, and we use them often. Not long ago, a kid was missing in the park. Somebody couldn't find their child, so we looked at the security cameras and found the kid hidden underneath someone else's camper, scared and really upset. Everyone was thankful that we were able to help.

In another example, somebody cut a hole in one of the glamping tents. By having cameras, we were able to find the responsible party. Those are just a few examples of why cameras are important to have.

Music

Whether it's at the pool, the office, or in a common area, a lot of times people want to play music. However, it's not legal to play music or movies unless you're specifically licensed for them. You can't play outdoor movies just because you happen to have a DVD or you bought the movie on Netflix or Amazon. You need a very specific license to play them for an audience.

You also can't play a radio station, Spotify, or any other form of music, even if you've purchased it, unless you have a special license to do that. Because these violations are serious offenses and can result in huge fines, I encourage you to do your homework here, and make sure you pursue the appropriate licensing for whatever plans you have regarding music and movies.

Air Filling

Having an air-filling station at your park is a nice feature, but it's not necessary. It is most appreciated in locations where there are a lot of cyclists, tubers, or golf carts.

Propane

Propane stations are common in almost all RV parks. However, I own an RV park that isn't allowed to have a propane station due to city restrictions. In every other case, I provide this service. To this end, make sure you check with the city that you're in if you're buying a property that doesn't have a propane station already (whether that's an existing park or land you plan to develop). Some states also require that the people who fill propane are licensed. These laws differ from state to state, so be sure to research what is required for your area.

There are a couple reasons you want to offer propane filling, if it is possible. This will be an extra income source for you, and it's a service that your guests need. Depending on the type of camper that they have, their heat, water, and/or stove may run off propane. Because you offer propane refills on-site, your guests don't have to travel to find someone else who does this.

In the event you can't fill propane in your park, you can have an exchange station similar to what you might see at a gas station. The guests trade out their tanks with you, and you can have a company fill or exchange those tanks whenever you run low. Having a service like this, however, is a second choice. If possible, see if you can fill the propane in-house. The one park I own where we aren't allowed to fill on our own has the exchange tanks, but we also have a list of recommended places for people to visit if refills are needed.

Chapter 20

OFFERING OUTSTANDING CUSTOMER SERVICE AND HOSPITALITY

A s an RV park owner, you are in the hospitality business. Your top priorities are your guests and their comfort at your park. Even with all the rules, you want them to have a good time and feel like they were treated nicely.

This is the core of customer service, which merits its own chapter. In the following pages, I will lay out some tips and tricks about keeping your guests happy by training your employees to be courteous and professional.

Like it or not, we now live with internet, videos, and instant commentary at our fingertips 24/7. That makes a single poor interaction with a customer an immediate public liability, so customer service is now more important than it's ever been.

One Interaction Can Make or Break Your Reputation

It is imperative that you always keep this in mind. Word spreads quickly, both within the RV community and on the internet. As a result, one soured interaction can impact public perception of your entire park and business. Similarly, one customer's testimony of good customer service can potentially bring in a lot more guests. Unfortunately, people are far more likely to complain than to compliment, so do your best to eliminate any opportunity to complain. Train your staff on how to deal with conflicts, complaints, and guest questions. If your staff treat people with respect and are focused on assisting customers to the best of their abilities, your park will be golden.

Answering the Phone

No matter how much information you put on your website or automate your reservation process, you should expect customers to still call you. To be responsive to phone calls and questions, make sure you have multiple staff members working the phones. Train them to answer calls in a way where all callers receive the same information.

I train my employees to greet the caller by identifying the property and providing their name. For example, at my property in Pigeon Forge, Tennessee, my team greets guests with "Thank you for calling your Pigeon Forge/Gatlinburg Jellystone. This is [employee name]. How can I help you?" If you have multiple parks, it is especially important that you provide the city or address of your location. People may be calling you as they drive down the road, and it's not always easy for them to confirm they are calling the park they intended to call. Make sure your introductory conversation includes these details.

Something else to consider is where to house your office staff members who answer the phones. In some parks, foot traffic is slower, and front desk employees can likely handle answering phone calls between guests. However, at some of my parks, my team members cannot help the guests in front of them and manage calls simultaneously, so I hire some staff for reservation and call roles and put them in a remote office. I have that option because I own multiple properties. If you do not have multiple properties or remote workers, you can always have your reservation staff located somewhere else on-site. In either case, with busy parks, I recommend separating call services from front desk workers. Your business will look more professional if your staff can give full attention to the customers at hand rather than putting callers on hold or having customers wait in line while a team member addresses questions on the phone.

When you assign customer service tasks to your teams, make sure everyone has access to all the information they need. Both front desk workers and phone staff should have park information and reservation status available at their fingertips. You do not want to lose customers over something as simple as a lack of internal communication. This is one reason to use either a reservation platform or have a website with built-in reservation tracking. That way, your employees can maximize your business revenue while improving customer service.

Script for FAQ

Most of the information people call about should be on a frequently asked questions list. For example, one of my properties is in a tourist town with a trolley. The trolley goes all over town and takes tourists to different destinations. Sometimes lodging areas will request trolley stops so people can go straight from their hotel or campground to another destination. My park does not have a trolley stop inside, although it is near a trolley stop. For this reason, my staff is trained to never answer no to the common question "Is there a trolley stop at your park?" That response would make guests less likely to stay at my park. Rather, I have them reply with "The main terminal for the trolley stop is a five-minute walk from the entrance of the property." That response informs guests that the stop is nearby in a way that does not discourage their stay.

Other questions will be more generalized to all parks. For any question that may come your way, your employees should answer them the same every time. Consistent responses make your business more professional and prevent confusion. Consistent answers are also better for marketing purposes. Having each employee answer questions the same way creates trust in your business. Consistency also helps when a guest tries to argue with your workers about some situation. Let's look at a demonstration of these interactions.

Let's say that a customer is calling to ask about your pet policies. One staff member simply answers, "We allow them on leashes." Another responds, "We are very pet friendly. All we need from you are their vaccination records, and we ask that you keep our park clean by cleaning up after your pet and keeping your pet on a leash when it is outside your camper."

In this example, there is some conflict in the staff responses, which can lead to confusion and frustration between campers and the staff. Avoid this by ensuring that your crew members give the same information, even if it is in a slightly different order. Not only should that clear up confusion, but it also shows that your staff is uniformly knowledgeable and can answer questions thoroughly and efficiently.

One of the best ways to ensure uniformity is to create an employee FAQ sheet with answers. This gives them a handy reference in case they forget any information, and it saves time by giving them an easily accessible cheat sheet.

SOPs

Standard operating procedures (SOPs) are great ways to streamline your training and customer service. SOPs are similar to FAQ sheets; they ensure that staff do the work the same way every time so that your guests can have proper expectations each time they visit the park. I will provide a few examples, but your park is best served if you create SOPs specific to your property.

A few jobs you will want SOPs for are check-in and check-out, opening and closing your offices, escorting guests to their sites, and site cleanup. In all these cases, you need your employees to put in the same level of effort and complete the same tasks. Otherwise, your campground will appear less organized, which decreases your customer satisfaction and retention.

Think about a team member going above and beyond in every job for their assigned site while another worker only does the bare minimum. The sites will look inconsistent. Another example is a staff member who brings their best when checking in guests versus an employee who seems less than pleased to check in a guest. These varied experiences not only impact the first-time visitor, they can also lead to distrust among returning guests. People want to know what they are getting when they visit. A roll-the-dice experience will lead to less business and less revenue.

SOPs fix these inconsistencies. They are essentially checklists that show how to complete each procedure consistently. How you go about creating your SOPs is up to you and what you think will work best for your park. SOPs provide detailed steps that can serve as training for new employees, as well as consistency reminders for long-term employees. Overall, SOPs are extremely helpful in keeping the work structured and equal across employees, which keeps your campground operating professionally, and your guests satisfied with every staff member who assists them.

Park Walk-throughs

Whether you plan to operate the property by yourself, through a management team, or with your own staff, daily park walk-throughs are a must. These walk-throughs are similar to the site checks we discussed in Chapter 13. However, rather than primarily checking on guests and how well staff members did their work, park walk-throughs give you an opportunity to see what needs to be done to prepare for the day. These walks are in addition to site checks and should be done in the morning before your park gets busy. This allows you to see trash that may have been missed, rowdy guests, guests that should have checked out already, or even a tree limb that fell. Customers will appreciate that you are paying attention to the grounds several times a day.

For park walk-throughs, I have my management team start at 7:30 a.m., then we open the office at 8:00 a.m. Every morning, I have the team physically walk the main part of the property, rather than taking a car or golf cart. By walking, they can better observe anything that is out of place or needs mending or cleaning. After assessing the scene, my management team reports to the maintenance and cleaning crews with what tasks will need to be completed that day. Then, all my employees are ready to start their workday.

Depending on the size of your park, you may ask multiple staff members to participate in walking the property. At a huge resort, that means your housekeeping manager is walking part of the property, your office manager is walking another part, and your maintenance manager is walking yet a third portion. They'll take their notes on the property they walked, then compare them and divvy up the work to other staff members.

This means that your managers need to be familiar with the area they assess. They must know what items belong in their section and how everything is oriented. Storms can knock things over, damage parts of the property, and cause a muddy mess around the property. If your management does not catch these flaws at the beginning of the day, your staff will not know everything that they need to address that day. Missing these details could also lead to bad internet reviews, even if the flaw is a onetime thing.

Walk-throughs are critical to the operation of your park and maintaining an impeccable atmosphere for your guests. This simple daily act is one of the greatest ways to deliver outstanding customer service.

Escorting Guests

Another way you can make your customer service stand out is to escort guests to their sites. You'd be surprised how many times we receive compliments both immediately and in reviews simply because our staff took five minutes to escort a guest to their site.

Let's face it—navigating unfamiliar places is a challenge. We typically balance looking at a map and the road at the same time, and we often become a hazard to others and ourselves in the process.

Now imagine doing that with a forty-foot RV that you rarely drive, while navigating tight turns and blind spots galore. Turns are much wider in RVs than in most vehicles, and as far as you can tell, the back of yours might as well be in another zip code. You can't see it to save your life.

Add in trees, utility boxes, and unfamiliar grounds, and you've got yourself a treacherous maze. This is why I always have my staff members escort guests, and I suggest you do the same if you can possibly spare the employees.

There are customer-focused reasons to escort guests, as well as park-focused reasons. When you offer to guide a guest to their campsite, you've started the relationship with a kind gesture. It's like walking someone you just met to their car or opening the door for someone you don't even know. It's extremely considerate and won't be forgotten.

Ensuring that customers park their RVs safely and in the right spots protects the park's property as well as the property of other customers. When guests park in the wrong spots, your reservations will be thrown off, and subsequent guests can feel slighted when they find that their site has been taken. This impacts ratings and typically reflects on the perception of professionalism at the park.

Aside from this, moving RVs after guests have settled can consume huge amounts of employee time and can negatively impact the experience for other guests. Imagine waiting for a fully plugged-in RV to unhook the water, sewage, and power, all while another guest is holding up traffic, waiting for the site.

On top of all these considerations, the safety of your park is a significant issue. I've seen campers run over pedestals, hit picnic tables, and bump into golf carts in their struggles to park their RVs. It costs a lot of money to repair everything people hit.

Handing out park maps can be helpful, and I encourage you to do so. However, navigating a large vehicle through a park is difficult, even with a map. When you assist guests with a personal escort, they become more comfortable and focus their attention on the road ahead rather than on the map.

Yet another factor is how many people have newly joined the camping world in recent years. If you think navigating an unfamiliar location is difficult, try doing it with a lengthy, unfamiliar vehicle as well.

And of course, the challenges we've mentioned don't even consider the mental state of the guests. Some arrive exhausted because they've driven for hundreds of miles in a single day. Driving an RV requires your full attention and is probably one of the most taxing forms of driving you will ever try. You have precious cargo. You are driving a beast. And pretty much no one respects how long your braking distance is.

Plus, there's the mental state that results from having multiple people cooped up in a small space. On many occasions, I have witnessed a husband-and-wife team arguing over how to park the RV properly. Their predicament is often complicated because neither of them is familiar with reversing or parking a large vehicle. Insert a courteous employee, and everything changes. The guests also become courteous. They work with each other, and the tone is recast.

The Bottom Line

There are ample reasons to escort guests. If you think you can't afford to spare the employees to do so, remember that damages to your park add up quickly, as do complaints about how your [fill in the blank] was positioned in the worst place possible. After paying the price for a couple of years, I implemented a policy that every guest is escorted unless they arrive after hours. I still deal with some damaged property from people parking RVs at night when it is hard for them to see, but it's not as much as I paid when my staff stayed in the office.

Implementation

Here's how I have taught my staff to implement the escort process. When people check in at the office, one of the front desk staff members sends a short text to one of the maintenance team members to let them know that they should come to the front of the park to help the guest.

That worker typically drives over in a golf cart, waits for the guest to finish checking in, and then guides them to their specific site. Because this crew member also needs to instruct the driver to pull into the spot, they should have experience backing up and parking an RV. They must stand so they are visible in the side mirrors, and as the customer eases backward, the employee must know when the ideal position is achieved.

I also instruct my staff never to enter the guest's camper. You don't park it for them, and you don't go in it to check on something they see. This boundary should never be crossed. Aside from insurance having a fit if this were to happen, it doesn't set a professional tone. Instead, have employees direct parking from outside the camper. This type of service is more than sufficient to dramatically improve your customer satisfaction.

Preparing pizza for guests.

Deliveries

Yet another way to stand out with superb customer service is to have in-house food offerings. Sure, you will be competing with the numerous delivery services that currently exist, but you'd be surprised how many guests don't want to wait forty-five minutes or more for a delivery. You may have a small menu, but you have it available ASAP, and you even offer the advantage of letting customers see and smell it, which are compelling selling points.

At my parks, I offer food that is universally popular, such as pizza. Pizza is also an easy, sharable meal for people on vacation. One of my properties even has a pizza kitchen. Guests can call the office or use an app to order pizza, and my staff brings it to their site. It's a fast, convenient option for guests and almost no extra effort for me. And most importantly, it improves the customer experience at my park while simultaneously increasing our park's profits.

There are other deliveries you can capitalize on to offer great customer service while boosting profits. The main delivery requests outside of food include firewood and ice. Firewood is heavy and messy, which can be frustrating for customers to deal with. Putting some firewood on the back of a golf cart and delivering it to them is a great option. You can also do this with ice. When someone orders ice, your staff can grab a bag and quickly drive it over to the campsite rather than having the customer walk to pick it up and bring it back to their site, by which time their ice may be melted. Whenever guests call for anything, I have the staff mention the various other options that we would be happy to bring to them. Act as a one-stop shop for your guests.

Your job as a campground owner is to make your guests' experiences the best imaginable. People on vacation want to relax and not worry about leaving the park to pick up simple things like dinner or ice. You can—and should—easily provide these services. When you do, your customers are more likely to return to your park, and many of these extra touches end up in customer reviews. The benefits to your business are huge compared to the minimal effort it took to satisfy your guests.

Staffing Surveys

Another great way to improve customer satisfaction is to ask for guests' opinions. One way I do this is by providing a housekeeping survey. The survey lets customers answer questions about their satisfaction with the housekeeping service and cleanliness of their stay. Of course, guests who come in their own RV will not receive housekeeping questionnaires. But anyone staying in one of your hospitality options (glamping, cabins, etc.) should be offered the survey. At the top of the paper, I have the housekeeper write their name along with a short note such as "I cleaned your room, and I hope you had a wonderful stay." The survey includes questions about the cleanliness of their accommodation, how well it met their needs, and whether there were any areas we could improve.

As guests leave the park, part of their check-out procedure is to bring the filled-out questionnaire to the front desk.

I have found that these surveys are most effective when I challenge the staff to earn 100 percent satisfaction on the surveys every day for a week. If they succeed, I give them an extra $5 per survey that guests turn in. Despite the hard work they have to put in, housekeepers will clean the property even more thoroughly because they are motivated to earn the extra cash. If they receive any negative feedback on the surveys, they do not get a bonus.

There's an inherent challenge in the hospitality business: providing what the customer wants but still having time to prepare and transition between customers. It's even harder to strike this balance at an RV park. Guests on their way out will often push for later check-outs. Meanwhile, your arriving guests sometimes ask for early check-ins. Given these competing goals, it is important that you stick to the posted schedule and that you schedule the housekeeping staff in the most logical, efficient way. After all, most parks don't have the budget for the massive staff you might see at a hotel.

As soon as a visitor leaves, my team immediately gets to work on the site and prepares it for the next guest. For cabins, rented campers, and glamping tents, employees need to have enough time to change the bedding and clean all surfaces, especially the bathroom. Laundry and other duties can be done later once the highest-priority transition tasks are accomplished.

Posting and Staffing Your Office Hours

Another aspect of optimal customer service is the office hours you display and your staffing efforts during those office hours. You will likely have gaps between check-in and check-out times during which your office will be less busy. If possible, you should run a little leaner during this time, but make sure to keep the office open anyway. Few people appreciate a "Will return at [fill in the blank]" sign.

At smaller mom-and-pop parks, you can justify more limited office hours. A nine-to-five day is typical for these types of campgrounds, and your staff can stagger their lunch breaks during the less-busy midday hours when traffic is at a minimum.

When you have a large enough park to warrant it, I highly encourage longer office hours, such as 8:00 a.m. to 11:00 p.m. I also encourage splitting the shifts into morning, afternoon, evening, and late-night periods. This allows you to staff a far longer workday without paying overtime to your employees.

Staffing your office for the late shift makes a lot of sense. Your guests will likely maximize their days and check in late. Some opt to drive an extra hundred miles before calling it quits, and others may want to visit a local attraction before checking in. Regardless of the reason, late check-ins tend to be tired, hungry, or both. If your camp store or office is not open when they arrive, you'll miss out on the purchases they would make in your shop, restaurant, or snack bar. Moreover, you'll miss out on the personal greeting your staff can provide. In my experience, these nighttime exchanges and sales more than make up for the extra hours of labor.

Staff Demeanor

As I've already shared, staff should always be courteous and professional. Anything less and a guest will feel they aren't on vacation. But there's a second rule that's just as important: Eliminate chitchat about your personal life, particularly in front of guests. Scenes like this can make customers feel uncomfortable, as well as unimportant. Moreover, it signals unprofessionalism and a lack of focus on efficiency. Customers end up thinking, *You have time to talk, but do you have time to get your job done so I can get out of here?*

Employees should give their undivided attention to customers, which happens to be what you are paying them for and what guests expect. Personal conversations are best left for the break room or home. You should expect this of your park employees, and make sure to include it in training.

Unhappy Guests

Even with incredible customer service, dealing with an unhappy guest is inevitable. Given that fact of life, you also need a plan for how to handle the occasional upset customer. I recommend training on precisely this issue, while also having published rules and guidelines in place that can serve as a reference point for your staff during any conflict.

The first step to take is to anticipate your problems, and make sure your policies clearly address them. For example, a common complaint across all hospitality venues is that guests cannot receive a refund once the cancellation deadline has passed. And there's a simple reason for such a rule: At some point, the host is unable to recover the lost revenue. When a guest reserves a spot, they promise to show up. Unlike airlines that overbook flights, parks and hotels operate on the assumption that those who reserve a place will show up.

Unfortunately, this logic is not sufficient for some unhappy customers. That's why I make sure policies like this are clearly explained on our websites, in booking confirmations, and in the materials that are displayed and/or handed out at the office.

On top of well-documented policies, you should also identify at least one person in your office who is an expert in maintaining a polite demeanor when talking to irritated guests. Some people will still yell and argue no matter how well the policies are documented, and when you have an employee who can diffuse hotheads and convert anger into gentle understanding, make sure you use their talents. Treat them well! They are worth their weight in gold.

I once had someone come into the office demanding a refund because a spider was in their tent. They made such a fuss that the health department was pulled in. Upon a thorough inspection, however, the health department found the culprit: a ladybug. Sometimes, it takes tremendous patience and support to deal with an irrational mind.

In other cases, you simply have to redirect the anger and remove the guest from the audience of other customers. This happened when I had a customer scream about the lack of linens in their cabin. Rather than acting bewildered and defensive, my worth-her-weight-in-gold employee asked the guest to walk outside so that she could gather more information.

Once outside, she learned the story wasn't as awful as it was being portrayed. The customer apparently checked in just as the housekeeper was finishing preparations. The housekeeper said she would return with three more towels but didn't return promptly due to some more urgent duties. While the guest was at the office complaining, the housekeeper had returned with fresh towels. The "oversight" was greatly overblown.

I incorporate best practices for dealing with difficult customers in my employee training. Whenever possible, staff members should remove a potentially angry guest from others waiting in the office or on the phone, because you never know how everything will play out. If you see early signs of frustration, try to move the conversation elsewhere. Leading a visitor outside creates a space for you to continue the discussion calmly. Sometimes, the lack of an audience also redirects the guest.

No matter the complaint, your staff should be trained and supported so that policies can ultimately prevail over irrationality. Sometimes, the best customer service is exemplified by patiently listening to the complaint. But at the end of the day, the rules that the rest of the guests follow should also apply to the hotheads.

Hostile Guests

Hopefully this is an extremely rare event for you, but sometimes there's nothing a staff member can do to redirect an angry customer. At that point, things may escalate to hostility.

In these cases, I teach my staff that there is just one course of action left: call 911. I don't want anyone to tolerate verbal or physical aggression, and I value staff and park safety over anything else. Hostility should never be acceptable.

Chapter 21

MAXIMIZING YOUR RV PARK

Renting an RV is an extremely affordable way to take a vacation. Most RVs are not only cheaper than renting a cottage, hotel room, or suite at a resort, they also have the advantage of being mobile. From an investor's standpoint, renting RVs is a huge potential revenue stream. It also closes the accessibility gap for the people who want to experience RV travel but don't have one. In this era of on-demand services, RV rentals are no exception.

Peer-to-Peer Rentals

Many travelers insist on using peer-to-peer RV rental companies as opposed to the traditional way of renting. Companies like Outdoorsy, RVshare, and RVezy have established themselves as leaders in the peer-to-peer rental industry. I want to talk about these three services and explain more about each one in case you want to leverage these platforms yourself or if you anticipate other people using them at your park and campground.

Outdoorsy is the most well known of the three services. Renters use the Outdoorsy website and enter the criteria for their search. After they enter their location, date range, and price range, they browse through lists of available RVs that match their search. Some renters' applications might be subject to the approval process of the owner (rather than booking the trip instantly), but not all owners require this. Outdoorsy lets renters choose from three insurance plans: basic, premium, and ultimate. They also give renters the option to purchase damage protection for the inside of the RV, as well as cancellation protection in case they need to cancel their trip. Based on the owners and the RV, the renter is required to pay a refundable $100 to $500 security deposit two days prior to the rental period and will get it back about one week after their stay. Outdoorsy has a huge selection of rental options available across the United States, United Kingdom, Canada, and Australia. Many people build their entire business model on this site.

RVshare is another online peer-to-peer rental service; it's the Airbnb of the RV world. If you own an RV, you can list it for rent on RVshare, making supplemental income on top of the revenue from your regular customers. RV owners create listings, set their own rates and availability, then communicate with interested parties.

Both owners and renters need to complete a profile, which contains reviews from people they've rented to or from. However, unlike Outdoorsy, RVshare puts little to no emphasis on these profiles. Many users neglect to fill them out, leaving one party in search of information with little means of contacting the other. But the saving grace is the renters can privately chat with the owner to discuss the details of their stay, and RVshare offers a secure payment system, so no cash or credit card details are ever handed to strangers.

Some RVshare owners have certain requirements, such as being 25 years old, having a valid driver's license, having three years of driving experience, or passing an automated DMV background check. Some owners allow instant bookings, but the majority of users need to request to rent, then wait to be approved.[8]

Because RVezy is new to the United States, they don't have the widest selection of RVs. But renters who do find something they like will experience exceptional customer service. Searching through listings with RVezy is simple and easy. Users can also download the RVezy app and browse that way. The booking process with RVezy is pretty straightforward. While some rentals have an instant booking option, others require renters to contact the owner directly and wait for them to respond for approval (similar to RVshare). Once approved, it typically takes twenty-four hours to finalize the deal.

When searching for an RV, renters enter details like where they plan

---

8   "The Ins and Outs of RV Rental for Newbies," RVshare, April 3, 2024, https://rvshare. com/blog/rv-rental/#:~:text=How%20old%20do%20you%20have,create%20their%20 own%20age%20policies..

to take the RV and how familiar they are with using one. They then enter their payment details and pay a refundable security deposit of around $1,000. The deposit is refunded within one to three business days after their completed stay. They can also decide if they want extras, such as having the RV delivered to their home. RVezy also offers roadside assistance for $18 a day, which, in the case of emergency, covers towing, tire replacement, septic blockage removal, on-site mechanics, locksmiths, meals, hotels, and taxi reimbursement.

RVezy's cancellation policy is a bit stricter than that of other services. If a renter cancels their booking thirty days or more in advance of the trip, they will receive a full refund. If the booking is canceled between eight and thirty days of the booked date, users will only receive 50 percent of the cost. Bookings canceled within one week or less of the trip receive no refund. (If an owner cancels the booking, the renter receives full reimbursement of the incurred expenses.)

It's really exciting that services like these exist, because it proves that there is growth within the RV industry. This means that more people can experience RV parks, even if they don't own a camper. On top of that, services like these can bring in more money for your business if you have RVs that you can't rent yourself.

Keep in mind that you don't even have to use these services. I rent several RVs in my campground, and guests book them through my own websites; I do not use a third-party service.

Franchising Options

In the RV space, there are two different options for franchises: KOA, which has over 500 locations, and Jellystone, which has just over eighty. They're two very different business models, and I want to share information on both.

I've never owned a KOA, but some KOA owners truly bleed yellow. They have a cult following, they love the product, and most franchisees are super excited about it. They also have one of the best conferences that I've ever been to.

Your other option is a Jellystone franchise. Jellystone is based on the Warner Brothers character Yogi Bear. These are parks that typically have quite a few amenities, and their target market is families.

Some people find franchising to be a great way to enter an industry. Franchises can provide advantages and general recognition, but only you know what's the best fit for your business.

Chapter 22

WHEN YOU SHOULD RETAIN PROFESSIONAL SERVICES

When you're on a budget, I know it's tempting to do a lot of things yourself, but it's not always the best idea. There are some areas of your business that will need to be outsourced to industry-specific experts. Let's talk about some of those, because I know that in the early years, when you're on a tight budget, sometimes you have to pick and choose what makes the most sense to hire out.

Niche Insurance

When it comes to insurance, if you don't make the right decision, you could be paying way more money than you should. When I bought my first park, I went with a local insurance company that was willing to insure the property. I had no idea that there was niche insurance. It took me a couple years of meeting other park owners to figure out that I was massively overpaying. Once I switched, I saved thousands of dollars per year.

Whenever you can, use industry-specific experts for insurance. You'll save yourself heartache and money.

Pest Control

Next up is a subject no one wants to hear about or speak about: bedbugs. If you're using alternative accommodations, it's not *if* an infestation will happen but *when* it will happen. Let's talk about what to do when that time comes.

There are not a lot of preventive measures you can take to prevent bedbugs. Eggs take between six and nine days to hatch,[9] so the people who discover bedbugs are not likely to be the same people who brought them in. When someone finds bedbugs, don't be surprised. Your heart will sink because they will likely put it on social media, so you've got to have to plan in advance for this.

Most likely those who find the bedbugs will want to check out immediately, and that specific unit needs to be nonoperational until you can get a pest control service out there. They need to be available to solve the problem within a couple of hours. Otherwise, you will lose a lot of money and get a lot of bad reviews. You must be prepared for when an infestation happens, because with so many guests coming and going, it's inevitable. For this reason, I enter into a service contract with a pest control company so that there is a defined amount of time by which they need to respond to my service requests.

Industry-Specific Attorneys

There are plenty of hazards of owning an RV park, and that's why legal advice can keep you out of trouble. What could you be sued over? Anything. A guest trips on a rock. A limb falls on a camper or tent. Someone drowns in the pool. A guest's dog attacks another guest. Someone is hit by a car. Regardless of the fact pattern you can imagine, there are hundreds of situations that could cause a lawsuit. That's why you need an attorney to review your various agreements.

There are some straightforward examples where you will need legal assistance as well. If you own a long-term park, make sure an attorney helps write your lease. Short-term parks may also need waivers for riskier things, like golf carts and pets. Make sure you consult someone who understands the industry, so you get adequate protection for the numerous potential liabilities that exist in your park.

---

9   Dini Miller and Andrea Polanco, "Bed Bug Biology and Behavior," Virginia Department of Health, December 12, 2014, https://www.vdacs.virginia.gov/pdf/bb-biology1.pdf.

Industry-Specific Accounting

Operating a campground is often a family dream, and you'll be an important part of building a lifetime of memories for your guests. But that glamorous picture changes when we talk about how to earn a decent living without losing a fortune to Uncle Sam.

Once again, I am not a tax expert. Therefore, I recommend you use an accountant who has experience in the RV industry. There are specific tax implications that RV park investing triggers, and you want to make sure you use a professional who is familiar with all of them. Some of the unique aspects of RV park investing are as follows.

Minimizing Tax Liability—Depreciation

There is a powerful tax-saving strategy available to those who invest in RV parks: depreciation. Your tax advisor and/or accountant will be able to show you all the ways you can depreciate a property and its assets. Depreciation is a common tax deduction that accounts for the wear and tear on structures, and it can save you thousands of dollars in taxes.

Although this list is not comprehensive, it includes some of the things you can depreciate over a shorter period than the replacement-cost period of thirty-nine years. Once again, you need to work with a tax professional on all of these matters.

- Picnic tables
- Splash pad areas
- Playground equipment for children
- Landscaping (trees, bushes, and shrubs)
- Land improvements, such as fences, lighting, drainage, paved parking areas, roads, etc.

One of the things about RV parks that I really like is that the assets found in an RV park can be reclassified and their depreciation accelerated at a much faster rate—possibly more than 50 percent faster. Let's help this sink in with a little math. What was your last real estate purchase? Subtract maybe 20 percent for land, which cannot be depreciated. Divide the remainder by fifty, and that's what you'd be able to write off in one year.

Let's say you spent just $250,000 purchasing an RV park. After deducting the land value (approximately $30,000), you found that $134,000 of the remaining value was short-term assets that could be depreciated over five or fifteen years. The current laws allow an owner to depreciate those assets over time or depreciate all of them in the first year. If they were unable to depreciate all the assets that year, the owner could continue to roll that depreciation forward. So, it's not a one-and-done scenario; that $134,000 stays around until you use it up.

Cost Segregation

Whether you own a residential rental house, an office building, or an RV park, another factor that is extremely important to your tax obligation is cost segregation. There are various assets that comprise the total value of your purchase, such as the building, the land it's built on, and other features and equipment. Cost segregation can identify those other assets and assign them a separate value and depreciation time frame; sometimes they can be depreciated over a shorter amount of time. As an example, carpet is something that you'll replace multiple times if you own a residential rental home. It's not going to last the twenty-seven-and-a-half years that applies to most rental properties, no matter how well you maintain it. So, why not take the value of that carpet and depreciate it over its useful life? That's what cost segregation allows you to do.

Be sure to find a tax professional who is familiar with the RV industry, as they would know best how to do a cost segregation and maximize your tax deductions. You'll find that you save more by doing this than you would trying to figure it out yourself. The bottom line is depreciation is a significant tax deduction, and you should make sure your tax professional is qualified to maximize this benefit to owning a park.

One of the myths I frequently hear is that if you don't do cost segregation in the first year, then you're ineligible to do it in the future. That couldn't be further from the truth. I know a park owner who purchased an RV park in 1996 for almost $17 million. In 2020, after twenty-four years, the owner still had almost $5.5 million that could be written off. So even if you purchased a property years ago, its potential for depreciation is still worth investigating.

Another owner I know purchased an RV park in 2018 for $4 million. After removing the value of the land ($1.7 million), they were able to reclassify 80 percent of the $2.3 million property valuation into five- or fifteen-year assets and rent the assets out in 2018. If they didn't use all that depreciation in 2018, it continues to roll forward until it's completely used up. This is a huge benefit. It's one of the powerful things about cost segregation and RV parks.

Let's review one more example. Let's say that you decide to upgrade your gravel pads to full cement or asphalt pads. As you might expect, this will cut down on maintenance and make the park more attractive. By segregating the gravel pad, you can write it off the year it is removed. Plus, you can write off the cost of having it removed. When you install the new pad, you can depreciate it in that same year. Each of these segregated items will be a huge benefit to your taxable income. The bottom line is there are many ways to deduct your expenses from your tax liability. Find an industry professional to help you navigate this process.

Installing cement pads.

Chapter 23
DON'T FORGET ABOUT MINDSET

I am often asked about being an entrepreneur and how I find ways to deal with the ups and downs, the successes and failures, and the moments that hurt so much that I almost want to give up. This book would be unfinished if I didn't offer a few thoughts on these subjects.

Facing Obstacles

Let me start by sharing the biggest obstacle I have ever faced. Just over ten years ago, I was pregnant with my third child, I was going through a divorce, and I was somehow given the opportunity to operate a previously failed RV park. I was an emotional mess, and when I look back, I'm sure God was involved in getting me through this period. Life was anything but stable.

The most prominent thought I had at the time was, *Can I do this? Really?* Day after day, I truly wondered if I was going to make it. Doubt crept in, and I wasn't sure I could do things by myself. And I hadn't yet figured out the "how"—how was I going to make this a success?

I remember thinking about moving home to live with my parents. I'd have more help if I did that. I would be stable. Life would be predictable.

That home happened to be in Illinois, and I have to be honest here—I *hate* the cold. Had they lived in Hawaii or Florida, I might be writing a different book. But Illinois? Whew. That was one big disincentive.

But thankfully, that move never happened, and something bigger was happening.

I was starting to realize that even though I was uncertain—even though I woke up doubting I could make it through this period—one thing was absolute: I was in control of my own life. If I wanted something, the only person stopping me from achieving it was me.

That realization is something I wish for everyone. I certainly wish that for you. Once you appreciate the awesome power of being in control of your own destination, no matter what obstacles stand in front of you, you begin to approach risk differently. You embrace it. Sure, it won't always work out. But *you* get to make the decisions, and *you* get to learn how to do things better. I wouldn't trade that for any opportunity to run back to safety.

That first RV park investment became one of many success stories that allowed me to build my real estate portfolio. I learned to thrive in the chaos of my personal life and entrepreneurship—a huge skill needed when you are an entrepreneur—and six years later, I was remarried and pregnant with my fifth child.

And on top of all of this, I homeschool my kids. But let's give credit where its due: I have an incredible team who helps me. I would not be able to do everything I pack into my days without my team.

My Greatest Takeaway

When I look back, this period gave me a new outlook on adversity. I learned that no one can help you better than you can help yourself. How do you help yourself? First, stop thinking of all the problems and issues that you face. Realize that every one of them is an opportunity. That hurdle you see? It's just a blip on your journey to success. In many ways, those hurdles create success for you.

If you look ahead and feel overwhelmed, you will give up. You'll think about how much effort it takes to succeed. Instead, focus on how much you can learn during the process. Approach every day as a learning experience—a journey toward being better—and the hurdles start to disappear. They become stepping stones instead—crucial parts of your journey that had they not been there, the journey would not have been complete.

What I used to view as obstacles I now view as part of life and business. Instead of dwelling on problems and issues, I deal with them head on. I enjoy the fact that I am living the life I want the way I want to live it. You have so many choices in life. Which path will you take? I prefer mine to have stepping stones. It is so much more interesting.

My Daily Routines for Mental Clarity

Many successful people have routines to start their days. They get up, exercise, do positive reinforcement, etc. My morning routines are more about others than they are about me. I'm raising and homeschooling three kids. So instead of a morning routine, I shift my routines to other parts of the day.

My first routine is at night. Before I go to bed each night, I think about and plan exactly what I want to accomplish the next day. (If you can't visualize it, how do you expect it to happen?) By mentally framing the following day, I can put my mind to rest and have a clear palette to work with the next day.

Second, I try to go on walks to the beach every day. A few years ago, I moved to Florida, because I wanted to be able to walk to the beach. The beach, the outside air, and the sound of the water give me much-needed space to find peace in my own thoughts without any distractions. In contrast to my evening routines, I let go of the present and my stressors as much as possible.

If you don't happen to have a beach nearby, you can accomplish the same type of distraction-free space in your backyard, in the woods, or perhaps by walking around the neighborhood. Some people say they carve out a space in their house where they can effectively block out everyone else. I haven't been so lucky.

Regardless of the locale, I believe the thoughts, ideas, and solutions that come to me when I have time to be alone are the best ideas of all. I encourage you to try it. Perhaps the creative juices flow better when you are sitting still, meditating in peaceful tranquility. Or perhaps you are like me, and the movement of walking helps generate ideas and solutions. Either way, the routine of seeking mental clarity has become an essential part of my day, and I hope it will be that impactful for you as well.

Staying Focused

One of my favorite books is *The Gap and The Gain*. In it, authors Benjamin Hardy and Dan Sullivan discuss a British Olympic rowing team who had never won a gold medal. However, as they approached their final Olympic regatta, the team quit training the way it always had. Instead, before every single decision the team made, the members asked themselves, *Will it make the boat go faster?* If the answer was no, then the decision (how they trained, what they ate, how late they stayed out) was made for them. Despite coming into the event as underdogs, they pulled through to win gold.

I apply this thought process in both my business and my personal life daily. Does this make the boat go faster? I also teach my kids to do this. Each day, I ask them if what they are doing makes the boat go faster. Are they distracted by a shiny, new thing, or does this continue them on their path—making their boat go faster?

Each decision you make, I want you to ask the same question: Does this make the boat go faster? Each opportunity that comes across your desk, every event you consider attending, every time someone asks for your time—does this make my boat go faster?

Celebrating Success

I'm sometimes asked how I celebrate success, and the truth is I celebrate it every day. I acknowledge when goals are met, and it gives me a sense of accomplishment. But I don't celebrate like most people do. I don't plan a party. I don't take vacations. Instead, I have been given the opportunity to live the life I want every day. This business has given me that.

I am so grateful, with all that God has given me, that I choose to enjoy those graces every day. I have that piece of chocolate whenever I want. And each day is a blessing to me.

My Personal Mantra

I can still hear it in my mother's voice: "Don't say 'I can't.' Say 'I can,' and do it." (Admittedly, my mother pounded it into my head, so how could I forget?) I'd feel challenged and say I couldn't do something. This was her response. Every time.

It had a lasting impact, because I learned to take action—today. So many people go their entire lives saying they are going to do something, but they never do it. They find excuses. Or they mull it over and discuss it some more.

Don't talk. Just do. The rest will follow.

The greatest reward is to see something that you worked so hard to build become bigger than you ever imagined. Take that first step. Get back up when you fall. And embrace the journey. I'll see you there.

CONCLUSION

Congratulations! You've made it to the end. At this point, we have walked through your entire experience—from thinking about the type of park that would best reflect your interests, to detailing what to look for in a deal and how to get funding, and what to expect once you are operating your own park. This foundational knowledge will allow you to begin your RV park and campground investing journey.

I hope I have also demonstrated the importance of going through this process with a team. No one can be an expert in everything, and I can certainly attest to the fact that leaning from industry experts is hands down the best way to avoid headaches. Look for professionals who know the RV park industry well—whether they are attorneys, Realtors, accountants, or maintenance personnel. And then engage others to help you with social media, assuming you aren't already an expert in that regard.

With a great team in place and with this book, you can master the granular operational components of being an RV park owner. You know what systems and processes you need in place, and you know what it takes to run a successful business. You are also getting my best advice on what software and tech pieces can lighten the load of daily operations. This means you are prepared to dive in and make the most of your investment. Running an RV park isn't as easy as many people think it is, but now you have seen how layered—and interesting—the journey can be. You will soon learn you have everything it takes to solve problems that might come your way.

Finally, I wish for you to experience all that I have experienced: the freedom to work for yourself, through an expression of yourself, that can ultimately be wildly successful and rewarding. I've been approached about countless other investments, and I continue to feel blessed that my journey led me here. The RV park investment path can be challenging at times, but it can also be a blank slate for your personality to shine, with unique and fascinating turns along the way. I look forward to hearing how your journey goes as well.

If you have any questions at all, please feel free to email me at info@ HeatherBlankenship.com.

ACKNOWLEDGMENTS

Real Estate Campgrounds reflects the journey and experiences I have been blessed to have by owning real estate, none of which would have been possible without the blessings from God and the cooperation and understanding of my entire family. I am humbled by how much I have been a student of the process, but at the same time, I am excited about what the future holds.

I want to take this opportunity to thank the many people who have been instrumental to my voyage, including several who made sacrifices with me. My successes would not have been possible without the support and contributions of countless friends, employees, contractors, and tenants, specifically Robbie Giles, Gail and Randall Dodd, Sandy Crawford, and Mike Haverstick. To my ex-husband, for not holding me back when I decided to impulsively buy something I knew nothing about. After that, the six years of hustling as a single mom made me who I am today. To my selflessly supportive husband, Josh, who now helps me hold down the fort at home, so I can continue to do something I love so much and provide for our family at the same time. Writing a book would not have been possible without the encouragement and support of my marketing team, Danny Miller and Jonathan Lang and Chris Haigh, who helped me turn a decade of knowledge into a tool to help so many others.

And by far, my greatest appreciation goes to my mother, Sherry Koebler, who has left her career, been my strongest cheerleader, supported me through all of my crazy ideas, and now serves as my COO. I give her all the credit for the mantra she instilled in me at a young age that still plays out in my head: "Don't say 'I can't;' say 'I can' and do it." This philosophy carries me through the days that might otherwise seem daunting.

Finally, I want to thank you, the reader, for joining me on this journey. It takes a unique personality to look inside oneself and envision how you can express yourself in your business pursuits. It is an honor to have your acquaintance, and the potential to work alongside each other. I wish you the highest levels of success in this endeavor.

SUPERCHARGE YOUR REAL ESTATE INVESTING.

Get **exclusive bonus content** like checklists, contracts, interviews, and more when you buy from the BiggerPockets Bookstore.

Pillars of Wealth: How to Make, Save, and Invest Your Money to Achieve Financial Freedom by David Greene

Take the guesswork out of financial freedom with a strategy perfected by countless self-made millionaires.

www.biggerpockets.com/pillars

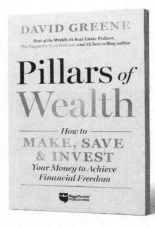

Start with Strategy: Craft Your Personal Real Estate Portfolio for Lasting Financial Freedom by David Meyer

Simplify your real estate goals with a portfolio plan that fits your personal values, resources, and skills.

https://store.biggerpockets.com/start-with-strategy

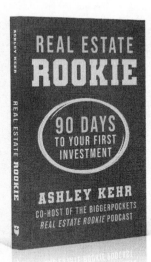

Real Estate Rookie: 90 Days to Your First Investment by Ashley Kehr

Ashley has helped thousands achieve real estate success, including listeners of the BiggerPockets Real Estate Rookie podcast and attendees of the Real Estate Rookie Bootcamp. Now, for the first time, she's bringing all that expertise in book form.

https://store.biggerpockets.com/ products/real-estate-rookie

Real Estate by the Numbers: A Complete Reference Guide to Deal Analysis by J Scott and Dave Meyer

From cash flow to compound interest, *Real Estate by the Numbers* makes it easy for anyone to master real estate deal analysis.

www.biggerpockets.com/ bythenumbers

Standard shipping is free and you get bonus content with every order!

www.BiggerPockets.com/STORE

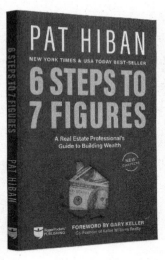

6 Steps to 7 Figures: A Real Estate Professional's Guide to Building Wealth by Pat Hiban

All the tactics that the best real estate agents use to become financially free and pursue the lives of their dreams.

www.biggerpockets.com/6steps

Set for Life, Revised Edition: An All-Out Approach to Early Financial Freedom by Scott Trench

Retire early from your nine-to-five and reach financial freedom with the actionable advice in this personal finance best-seller with more than 130,000 copies sold.

www.biggerpockets.com/setforlife

Standard shipping is free and you get bonus content with every order!

www.BiggerPockets.com/STORE